To _Morgan Rourke_

From _Sandy, with love_

_On her First Communion Day_

_May 6, 1989 (from Uncle Bob, too!)_

# THE DOUBLEDAY ILLUSTRATED CHILDREN'S BIBLE

# THE DOUBLEDAY ILLUSTRATED CHILDREN'S BIBLE

## BY SANDOL STODDARD
## PAINTINGS BY TONY CHEN

DOUBLEDAY & COMPANY, INC., GARDEN CITY, NEW YORK

## CONSULTANTS

Mary Ann Getty, RSM, Ph.D.,
Associate Professor of Theology at
Carlow College, Pittsburgh, Pennsylvania

Baruch A. Levine,
Professor of Hebrew, Department of
Near Eastern Languages and Literature
at New York University, New York, New York

Rev. Bruce M. Metzger,
Professor of New Testament Language
and Literature at Princeton Theological
Seminary, Princeton, New Jersey

Library of Congress Cataloging in Publication Data
Stoddard, Sandol.
  The Doubleday illustrated children's Bible.
  Summary: An illustrated retelling of more than
100 stories from the Old and New Testaments.
  1. Bible stories, English. [1. Bible stories]
I. Chen, Tony, ill.   II. Title.
BS551.2.S745   1983     220.9'505     82-45340

ISBN: 0-385-18541-3
LIBRARY OF CONGRESS CATALOG CARD NUMBER: 82-45340
COPYRIGHT © 1983 BY NELSON DOUBLEDAY, INC.
ALL RIGHTS RESERVED
PRINTED IN THE UNITED STATES OF AMERICA
BOOK DESIGNED BY DAVID NOVEMBER
ART DIRECTION BY DIANA KLEMIN
DELUXE EDITION

*For my grandchildren*
*Jesse Daniel, Emily Margaret*
*Lisa Sandol and*
*Samuel Mayer Warburg*

## AUTHOR'S NOTE

Although many commentaries and scholarly works have been helpful to me, I have relied primarily in this book upon *The Jerusalem Bible, The Holy Bible: Revised Standard Version,* and *The Holy Bible: King James Version.* My aim has been to make an extremely condensed but only slightly simplified rendering of biblical literature, presented as one continuous set of events, perceptions, and reflections into which the youngest of readers can enter with ease. Interpretive material has been kept to a minimum. The book is intended not as a collection of stories *about* the Bible, but as a pathway toward the power and mystery of that immortal work itself.

## ACKNOWLEDGMENTS

With special thanks not only to my editors, Barbara Greenman and Marjorie Goldstein; art director, Diana Klemin; copy editor, Frank Hoffman; advisors, Mary Cullen, Robert Heller and Eve Roshevsky; and our execellent team of consultants, but to the many friends and colleagues who have contributed to this work, especially: James H. K. Norton, who generously and patiently instructed me; Donn Morgan and Bill Eddy, who offered valuable suggestions; Ed Bonsey, Don Lyons, and members of my women's group, who ministered to me; Peter R. Goethals, who sheltered and encouraged me; and Sr. Martha Reeves, who prayed.

# Contents

11 OLD TESTAMENT

13 In the Beginning
GENESIS 1 - 3

18 Cain and Abel
GENESIS 4:1-18

21 Noah and the Flood
GENESIS 5 - 9:17

25 The Tower of Babel
GENESIS 11:1-9

29 Abraham: The Journey and the Covenant
GENESIS 10, 12 - 18

35 The Destruction of Sodom
GENESIS 19:1-29

37 Abraham and Isaac
GENESIS 21:1-9; 22:1-19

39 Isaac and Rebekah
GENESIS 24

41 Jacob's Story
GENESIS 25:19-34; 27:1-45; 28:10-22; 29 - 32

45 Jacob Meets an Angel
GENESIS 32:23 - 33:5

47 Joseph and His Brothers
GENESIS 37

50 Joseph in Egypt
GENESIS 39 - 46:7; 49

56 Moses
EXODUS 1:8 - 2:10

58 Moses and the God of Abraham
EXODUS 2:11 - 4:12; 5:1-14; 7 - 13

63 Crossing the Sea
EXODUS 14

64 The Cloud and the Fire
EXODUS 15 - 17:7; 19; 20; 24:12-18; DEUTERONOMY 5

71 The Golden Calf
EXODUS 32

72 Tabernacle of the Lord
EXODUS 25 - 31; 33 - 40; NUMBERS 9:15-23

77 Love and Law
EXODUS 22; LEVITICUS 1 - 7; 16; 19:34; 20; 23; DEUTERONOMY 12 - 25

79 Journeying Toward Canaan
NUMBERS 10:11-36; 11:1-30; 13; 14; 20

82 The Story of Balaam the Magician
NUMBERS 21 - 24

85 The Farewell of Moses
NUMBERS 27:12-23; DEUTERONOMY 1 - 4; 6 - 11; 29 - 34

89 Joshua and the Conquest of Canaan
JOSHUA 1 - 24

95 Deborah the Judge
JUDGES 4; 5

99 Gideon and the Midianites
JUDGES 6 - 8

103 Jephthah's Daughter
JUDGES 11

105 Samson
JUDGES 13 - 16; 21:25

109 Ruth
RUTH 1 - 4

112 Samuel
1 SAMUEL 1 - 7

**116 Israel Is Given a King**
1 SAMUEL 8 - 10:1

**118 Saul: A Troubled Monarch**
1 SAMUEL 10:2 - 15:31

**121 The Shepherd Boy**
1 SAMUEL 16:1-13

**123 David and Goliath**
1 SAMUEL 16:14-23; 17:1-52

**126 The Outlaw**
1 SAMUEL 18 - 24;
1 CHRONICLES 12

**131 The Witch of Endor**
1 SAMUEL 28

**132 David the King**
1 SAMUEL 31; 2 SAMUEL 1 - 12;
1 CHRONICLES 10 - 17

**139 David and Absalom**
2 SAMUEL 13 - 19; PSALMS 3

**141 Solomon's Glory**
1 KINGS 1:1-40; 3:1-15; 5; 6; 8; 9;
1 CHRONICLES 22; 28; 29;
2 CHRONICLES 1 - 9

**145 The Wisdom of Solomon**
1 KINGS 3:16-28

**147 The Queen of Sheba**
1 KINGS 10; 2 CHRONICLES 9

**149 The Song of Solomon**
THE SONG OF SONGS 1 - 8

**153 A Kingdom Divided**
1 KINGS 11; 12; 2 CHRONICLES
10 - 12

**155 Ahab and Elijah**
1 KINGS 17; 18

**158 The Story of Jonah**
JONAH 1 - 4

**161 Naboth's Vineyard**
1 KINGS 21

**163 Elijah and Elisha**
1 KINGS 19; 2 KINGS 2; 9:30-37

**166 Amos: The Angry Shepherd**
AMOS 1 - 9

**169 The Fall of the Northern Kingdom**
2 KINGS 16; 17; 2 CHRONICLES 28;
ISAIAH 7

**170 Isaiah of Jerusalem**
ISAIAH 1 - 39; 2 KINGS 18; 19;
2 CHRONICLES 32

**176 A Book Is Found**
2 KINGS 22:1-10; 2 CHRONICLES
34

**178 Jeremiah and the Fall of Jerusalem**
2 KINGS 23:28-30; 24;
2 CHRONICLES 35:19-25; 36:17-20;
JEREMIAH 1; 18; 36; 38; 52

**182 By the Waters of Babylon**
JEREMIAH 39; PSALMS 137

**184 Consolation and Prophecy**
JEREMIAH 29 - 32; 43; EZEKIEL 34;
37

**187 A Voice in the Wilderness**
ISAIAH 40 - 55

**193 Return to Jerusalem**
2 CHRONICLES 36:22, 23; EZRA 1;
3; 7 - 10; NEHEMIAH 1 - 6; 8

**196 Job**
JOB 1 - 42

**201 The Story of Esther**
ESTHER 1 - 10

**203 The Fiery Furnace**
DANIEL 1 - 4

**206 Belshazzar's Feast**
DANIEL 5

**208 Daniel and the Living God**
DANIEL 6 - 12

**211 Psalms**
THE PSALMS 1 - 150

**218 Between the Old Testament and the New**

**223 NEW TESTAMENT**

**225 Time of Miracles**
JOHN 1:1-14; LUKE 1:26-56

**228 The Child Is Born**
MATTHEW 1; 2; LUKE 2:1-40; 3:23-38

**235 Boy in the Temple**
LUKE 2:41-52

**236 John the Baptist**
LUKE 1:5-25, 57-80; 3:1-22; JOHN 1:19-34; MATTHEW 3:1-17; MARK 1:1-11

**239 Temptation**
MATTHEW 4:1-11; MARK 1:12-13; LUKE 4:1-13

**241 Lamb of God**
JOHN 1:29-51; 2

**245 The Fishermen**
MATTHEW 4:18-22; MARK 1:16-20

**247 Stranger in His Own Land**
MATTHEW 4:12-17; 7:28-29; 13:54-58; MARK 1:14-15, 21-28; 6:1-6; LUKE 4:14-30

**251 My Father's House**
JOHN 2:13-25; MATTHEW 21:12, 13; MARK 11:15-19; LUKE 19:45-48

**253 The Woman at the Well**
JOHN 4:1-42

**257 The Sermon on the Mount**
MATTHEW 5 - 7; LUKE 6:20-49; 11:1-4, 9-13; 13:23, 24; 14:34, 35; MARK 4:21; 9:50; 11:25, 26

**263 A Storm Is Stilled**
MATTHEW 8:23-27; LUKE 8:22-25; MARK 4:35-41

**264 Healer of Galilee**
MATTHEW 4:23-25; 8:5-13, 16, 17; 9:1-13, 18-26; 11:18, 19; 12:46-50; MARK 1:32-39; 2:1-12; 3:1-6, 31-35; 5:21-43; LUKE 4:40-44; 5:17-26; 6:6-11; 7:1-10, 24-35; JOHN 4:43-54

**269 Seeds and Treasures**
MATTHEW 13; MARK 4:1-34; LUKE 8:4-18

**273 Twelve Are Chosen**
MARK 6:7-13; LUKE 9:1-6; 10:1-16; 14:26, 27; MATTHEW 9:35 - 10:39

**276 Death of a Martyr**
MATTHEW 14:1-12; MARK 6:14-29; LUKE 9:7-9

**279 The Pool of Bethesda**
JOHN 5:1-18

**281 Food for the Hungry**
LUKE 8:1-3; MATTHEW 14:13-21; 15:1-20, 32-39; MARK 6:30-44; 7:1-23; 8:1-10; JOHN 6:1-15

**285 A Different Kind of King**
JOHN 6:22-69; 8:12-59; MATTHEW 16:13-23; 17:1-8; MARK 8:27-33; 9:2-8; LUKE 9:18-22, 28-36

**291 Faith That Moves Mountains**
MATTHEW 17:14-21; MARK 9:14-29; LUKE 9:37-43

**293 Children of God**
LUKE 9:46-48; 17:1-3; 18:15-17; MARK 9:33-37; 10:13-16; MATTHEW 18:1-14; 19:13-15; JOHN 3:3

**295 The Good Samaritan**
LUKE 10:29-37; MATTHEW
25:31-46

**298 Eye of the Needle**
LUKE 13:31-33; 16:19-31;
18:18-30; MATTHEW 8:20;
19:16-30; MARK 10:17-31

**302 Mary and Martha**
LUKE 10:38-42

**304 The Prodigal Son**
MATTHEW 11:28-30; 18:12-14;
LUKE 7:36-50; 15:11-32

**308 The Man Born Blind**
JOHN 9:1-28

**310 Mercy and the Law**
JOHN 8:1-11

**312 Lazarus Raised**
JOHN 11

**315 Day of Joy**
MATTHEW 21:1-9; MARK 11:1-10;
LUKE 19:28-38; JOHN 12:12-19

**317 Jerusalem, Jerusalem**
MATTHEW 22 - 25; LUKE 10:25-28;
12 - 14; 19:11-44; 20; MARK
12:1-35; JOHN 18:14

**321 The Last Supper**
JOHN 13 - 17; MATTHEW 26:17-36;
MARK 14:1-31; LUKE 22:1-34

**327 The Garden of
Gethsemane**
MATTHEW 26:30-56; MARK
14:26-50; LUKE 22:39-53; JOHN
18:1-11

**330 Trial and Agony**
MATTHEW 26:57 - 27:44; MARK
14:53-72; 15:1-32; LUKE 22:54-71;
23:1-43; JOHN 18:12 - 19:27

**335 Death and
Resurrection**
MATTHEW 27:45-66; 28; MARK
15:33-47; 16; LUKE 23:44-56; 24;
JOHN 19:28 - 20:29

**340 Birthday of the
Church**
MATTHEW 28:16-21; MARK
16:12-20; LUKE 24:13-53; JOHN
20:30 - 21:25; ACTS 1 - 5;
1 CORINTHIANS 15:1-7
ACTS 6; 7

**346 On the Road to
Damascus**
ACTS 8:1-3; 9:1-19; 22:6-21;
26:12-16; GALATIANS 1:11-24

**349 Sowing of the Seeds**
ACTS 8:4-8, 26-40; 9:20-25;
10:9 - 11:18; 2 CORINTHIANS
11:30-33

**354 What Gods Are
These?**
ACTS 11:19-26; 12:1-19; 13; 14

**357 Council at Jerusalem**
ACTS 15:1-29

**359 Mission to Greece**
ACTS 16:19-40; 17:16-34; 18:1-11;
20:7-12; 1 CORINTHIANS 1:17 -
4:13; 2 CORINTHIANS 10:1-10;
11:23-28

**363 Riot at Ephesus**
ACTS 19:23-41

**365 Prison on a Hilltop**
1 CORINTHIANS 1:10-14; 6:19-21;
12; 13

**369 If God Be With Me**
ACTS 20:17-38; ROMANS 8:31-39

**371 Appeal to Caesar**
ACTS 21 - 26

**375 Voyage to Rome**
ACTS 27, 28; 2 TIMOTHY 4:6-8

**380 Revelation**
THE BOOK OF REVELATION 1 - 22

# THE OLD TESTAMENT

# In the Beginning

In the beginning, when God made heaven and earth, the world that we know had not yet come into being. There was nothing at all anywhere except a great emptiness and a living spirit which was God, moving as a mighty wind moves over dark waters.

God said, "Let there be light!" and there was light. He saw that the light was good, and he separated it from the darkness, calling the light *day* and the darkness *night*. This is what happened on the first day; and then the evening came, and then the morning.

Next, God shaped the sky to curve over the earth like a vaulting dome, and he called the dome *heaven*. This is what happened on the second day; and then the evening came, and then the morning.

Now God said, "Let the waters under heaven be gathered into one place, so that there will be dry land!" God called the dry land *earth,* and the gathering places of the waters he called *seas.* "Let there be plants on earth," he said, "and trees of many kinds, each bearing its own seed!" And so there were, and God looked at all of this work he had done, and he saw that it was good. And the third evening came, and then the morning.

On the fourth day God made the sun and the moon and the stars. He placed them in heaven to bring light to the earth, and to show us how to measure time and the seasons; and he saw that this was good. So the fourth evening came, and then the morning.

And on the fifth day God said, "Let the waters be filled with living creatures, and let there be birds in the air of heaven!" So he made all sorts of fishes, great and small, and he made sea monsters and every kind of bird. God saw that this was good, and he blessed them, telling them to multiply, for God wanted the waters and the air of his new world to be filled with life. This is what happened on the fifth day; and then the evening came, and then the morning.

On the sixth day, God said, "Let the earth produce living creatures! Let there be wild animals and cattle and reptiles of every kind!" And so there were, and God looked at all the life he had created; and he saw that it was very good. He blessed the animals, telling them that they should give birth to many more creatures like themselves, each of its own kind.

Now, God was pleased with all of his work, but he was not entirely satisfied, for there were no human beings yet. So God made man and woman with spirits like his own, in order that they might come to know him, and to love the beautiful world he had been making. And the evening came, and then the morning; and on the seventh day, God rested.

The name of the first man was Adam, and the name of the first woman was Eve; and this is how God made them. First he made Adam out of the dust of the earth. And then, while Adam slept, God took a rib from his side and shaped from that the body of Eve.

"Bone from my bones,
Flesh from my flesh,"

said Adam when he first saw Eve; and he loved her, not as a creature separate and strange, but as a part of himself. In the same way, Eve loved him. And so the first man and the first woman began their lives at peace with one another and with all creation. God brought the animals to Adam one by one, and Adam named them all. The fruits of the earth were everywhere for Adam and Eve to eat; the air around them was warm and comfortable; and they wore no clothes, not feeling any need for them.

Now, God had planted a garden eastward in Eden where four great rivers flow; and in this garden he had put every kind of fruit that was beautiful and good to eat. In the center of the garden stood the Tree of Life, and beside it stood the Tree of Good and Evil. "Take care of this garden," God told Adam and Eve, "and eat any fruit that you wish, except the fruit from the Tree of Good and Evil. If you eat that, you will surely be doomed to death."

But in the Garden of Eden there was an evil spirit which had taken the form of a serpent, and he was the wickedest of all the creatures God had made. This serpent knew that God alone has the power to decide what shall be good and what shall be evil in the world, and he was jealous of God. "Eat this fruit," the serpent whispered to Eve. "You will not die from it. You will gain power like God's to know and to do whatever you please without punishment." So Eve ate some of the fruit, and then she gave some to Adam, and he ate also. A moment later they realized for the first time that they were naked; and they felt ashamed, so they covered themselves with garments made of fig leaves.

Then they hid themselves away from God; and they heard him walking in the garden in the cool of the day. "Where are you?"

God called to them. "What have you done?" Adam answered, "I was hiding because I was ashamed. The woman gave me the fruit you said was forbidden, and I ate some of it." God asked Eve, "What have you done?" and she said, "I tasted the fruit also, because the serpent tempted me."

Now God was angry indeed. He placed a curse upon the serpent's evil spirit, naming it as the eternal enemy of mankind. "You shall crawl upon the ground from now on," he said, "and the offspring of this woman shall crush your head."

"You must leave this garden paradise," God told Adam and Eve. "You have taken the one fruit that I forbade you, and from now on your life will be very different and very hard. You must grow your own food in the future, by the sweat of your brow. You must labor and toil to give birth because of this, and some day you will grow old and die. I brought the life of man and woman out of the dust of the earth; and to dust you shall return." Adam and Eve turned away in grief to leave the garden, and God, feeling pity for them, gave them clothing made of the skins of animals, to protect them as they made their sorrowful way out into the world.

Thus the first man and the first woman betrayed God's trust in them. Although they did not know it yet, the love of their Creator would follow them into the wilderness and would remain with them, from that time on, wherever they might go. Yet their loss was great; and to guard his Tree of Life forever, God placed angels with flaming swords at the gates of Paradise.

# Cain and

Now Adam and Eve toiled together in the land beyond Eden. In time a son was born to them; they named him Cain. How Eve rejoiced! "With the help of God," she said, "I have brought a man into the world!" Cain grew and thrived, and then another son was born, who was named Abel.

In times long ago it often seemed to people that their Lord God must be very far away indeed. Laboring in the wilderness, Cain the farmer and Abel the shepherd decided one day that God might look upon them with greater favor if they should offer him some gifts.

And so, to a holy place Cain brought food that he had grown

# Abel

in the hard, rocky soil, and he was very proud of his offering. His younger brother, Abel, brought a fine, fat lamb that was the firstborn of his precious flock. Each brother put his gift into a fire, so that the sweet-smelling smoke of it would rise to heaven and attract the notice of the Lord.

Now something happened that neither of the brothers could understand, for it was one of God's mysteries. He made it known to them that he was well pleased with Abel and his offering but that he did not look with favor upon Cain or upon Cain's gift. At this, Cain became furiously angry. He went away and walked alone under the sky, brooding.

The Lord came after Cain and told him, "Lift up your head!

Why are you so jealous and hateful toward me? You are thinking of nothing but your pride, and the urge to sin waits like a beast by the door to devour people at such times. You must be master of it!"

But Cain had no room in his heart to receive these words; he was filled with rage and he continued to brood. Finally, walking one day in the fields, he turned suddenly upon his brother, Abel, and killed him. So was the world's first murder done in the fury of hurt pride and in the terror that comes upon people when they separate themselves from God.

The Lord came looking for Cain yet again and asked him, "Where is your brother, Abel?" Cain lied. "I do not know where he is," he replied. "Am I my brother's keeper?"

"What have you done?" God asked Cain. "Listen to the sound of your brother's blood crying out to me from the ground! Do you think this earth will grow anything good for you, after such a deed? No! There shall be a curse upon you, and you shall be driven away from this place."

Cain wept. "If I must be homeless, and a wanderer upon the earth," he said, "anyone who finds me will be sure to kill me!" So the Lord put a special mark of protection upon Cain, to help him dwell in safety. And after this, Cain went away to the land of Nod, where he found a wife and had children; and in time, he built a town of his own.

# Noah and the Flood

**B**y now, people had become plentiful upon the earth, and God was sorely distressed, seeing that they continued to do wicked things. At last he thought, I am sorry I ever made these human beings. My lovely earth is filled with violence on their account. It is time for me to do away with them.

But there was one good and righteous man on earth, named Noah, and the Lord thought very carefully about him. The Lord told Noah, "I will offer you a covenant. I am going to make it rain for forty days and forty nights, and the waters of the flood will rise until every living thing on earth is killed. But you are a good man, the only one of your generation, and I promise I will not let you die. And your wife will not perish, nor your sons, nor your sons' wives." Noah had three sons, named Shem, Ham, and Japheth.

The Lord told Noah what to do. "You must make an ark," he said. "Build it four hundred fifty feet long and put a strong roof on it. Give it three decks, and a door that opens high up on the side. Bring plenty of food into the ark to feed yourselves and the creatures I want you to take with you."

So Noah built the ark just as God had instructed him, and he made it ready in every way. "Now," said the Lord, "you must take two of every kind of animal with you, one male and one female so that they can give birth, in time, to more like themselves. I want

you to save in this way every animal I have made, and every
creature that crawls upon the ground, and everything that flies."

Noah did exactly as God had told him. The animals boarded
the ark together, two by two. Then Noah and his family went
aboard, and God shut the door of the ark behind them. This was
the seventeenth day of the second month of the six-hundredth
year of Noah's life. And it began to rain, and it rained and it rained
and it rained.

For forty days and forty nights the waters rose. The ark was
lifted until it sailed high above the ground, higher than the highest
mountaintop. In the flood below, the cattle died, and the wild
beasts, too. The birds and the insects died, and the reptiles died,

and so did every human being. Within the ark there was a great deal of noise and trouble, loneliness and fear. Yet Noah and his family were safe, together with two of every living creature that draws breath on earth; for in all this time, the Lord God had not forgotten them. At last, one day, he sent a mighty wind to blow the waters aside, and the ark came gently to rest on the top of Mount Ararat. Noah opened a window and looked out. As far as he could see, there was nothing but water.

So Noah sent a raven to explore. Back and forth the raven flew, but there was no dry land in sight. Next, Noah sent a dove, but he could not find a place to perch, and he came back at last to Noah's hand. Seven days went by, and Noah sent out the dove again. This time the little bird returned bearing in its beak an olive branch with new, green leaves. Noah knew, seeing this, that the worst of the danger was past. Again, however, he waited seven days. He sent out the dove once more, and this time it did not return. Now Noah opened the door of the ark at last, and he saw that the ground was dry. "Come out now," the Lord told them all. "Come out of the ark and begin a new life! Fill up the world again, and do no more violence and wickedness!"

Noah and his family came out to the dry land, and the animals followed. How good it was to see the earth again, and to walk upon it! The first thing Noah did was to build an altar there on the mountaintop and prepare burnt offerings in thankfulness to God for their survival.

Soon the Lord God noticed the fine fragrance rising up to heaven, and he said to himself, "I will never do such a thing again!" To Noah he said, "Walk in my ways and take care of my earth, for I mean people to be masters of it and of every living creature. From now on, human beings must obey my laws!"

And then, looking down upon Noah and his little band upon the mountaintop, the Lord God said, "Perhaps I shall always find evil wishes in people's hearts. Nevertheless, I will never punish my world with such a flood again. To you and your descendants, Noah, this is my promise—this is my covenant."

When he had heard these words, Noah looked up into the sky. There, like a mighty arch between heaven and earth, he saw a rainbow shining. That, he knew, would be forever a sign of God's covenant—a message from above, of love and peace.

# The Tower of Babel

After the flood, the sons of Noah had children, and then these children grew up and had children of their own. There were many famous people in those days who lived until they were very, very old. Cities such as Babylon and Nineveh began to appear; for, by now, the descendants of Noah had spread from the mountains to the deserts and the river valleys, and they had settled even upon the shores of the Mediterranean Sea. At this time, all of them were still closely related, and they all spoke the same language. It was easy for them to make great plans together, and to feel that they were very important indeed.

One day, in Babylon, the people found a new way of building things: They learned how to mix mortar, and to bake bricks. Seeing how easy it was to work with these bricks, they were extremely pleased with themselves. "Come," they said to one another, "let us make a tower that will reach all the way up to heaven! Then we can rise up so high that we will be just as important and powerful as God is, and everyone will be afraid of us!"

So they made a great many bricks, and then they began to build their tower. Day by day, higher and higher it went. The people became more and more impressed with themselves and more and more excited. If a man carrying bricks did not move quickly enough, the leaders whipped him and called him vile names. If a woman wanted to stop working so that she could take care of her children, they beat her and made her stay. All their thoughts were for the tremendous tower they were building, and for the way people would bow down to them when it was done.

The Lord God was watching all of this, and he was not pleased. "How proud and stupid these people are!" he said to himself. "The least thing they learn to do makes them think that they are gods. And now they are making a miserable place out of my earth all over again. What will they think of next, if I do not stop them?"

But God had noticed that these people were all speaking the same language, and that this made it easy for them to work together. "Let there be an end to that!" he said. "From now on, let there be different languages among all people and among all the tribes on earth!" Immediately, the people working on the Tower of Babel found that they could not understand one another. The words of one person were to another nothing but a babble of sounds. This frightened them all, and some of them ran away, bringing their strange, new languages with them to the faraway places of the world. Others stayed, but when their leaders ordered them back to work, no one could understand, so no one obeyed.

And now in all the land there was peace once more. Laughter and music were heard again. People took time to be kind to one another and to enjoy the beauty of the earth; and parents went home to their children and told them for many, many years afterward the story of the Tower of Babel.

# Abraham: The Journey and the Covenant

**A**fter the flood, the family of Noah had scattered far and wide. Japheth traveled north; Ham and his people moved to the south; and Shem went east to the place in Babylonia called Ur, where mighty rivers meet the sea. To the descendants of Shem, in time, Abraham was born; and he became a shepherd, a man known for his wisdom and for his virtue. Abraham's wife was Sarah, a strong and cheerful woman, noted for her great beauty. They had a comfortable life together, their only sorrow being that they had no child.

One day, the Lord God came to Abraham and said, "Leave this country! Go from here and I will show you another land. There I will make your people into a great nation and a source of blessing for all mankind. I will show you such favor that people will say forever after, 'May you be as blessed as Abraham!' "

Abraham did not hesitate. Immediately upon hearing this, he gathered together his family and his flocks; and with all his tents and his household goods, and with all his great wealth of gold and of silver, he left the place called Haran, in Syria, which had been his home. Westward he traveled with his people toward the country of the Canaanites; and Sarah went with him, and so did their nephew, Lot.

When they came to the banks of the river Jordan, Abraham

and his followers gazed with joy at the land of Canaan, for it was a place of rich, green pastures and meadows bright with flowers. "This is the land that I will give to your descendants," God told Abraham. So Abraham built an altar to the Lord there beside a great tree called the Oak of Moreh, and he offered up thanks.

Years of wandering lay ahead; Abraham and his people moved south to the Negeb for a time, and then, to escape a drought, as far as the land of Egypt. At last they returned to settle in Canaan, and still Abraham and Sarah had no child. "Take what land you choose," Abraham told Lot. "My people and I will go elsewhere." For, by now, they had so many possessions and so many followers that they could not all stay comfortably in the same place. Lot was tired of living in the open country, and he decided to pitch his tents at Sodom, which was a town well known for its luxury and wickedness. But Abraham knew it was wrong to live in such a place, and he took his people westward again, into the heart of Canaan's pastureland.

Here the Lord came once more to speak with him. "Look around you, Abraham," he said. "All of this land shall belong to your descendants someday, for you have kept faith with me." Abraham replied, "My Lord, what do you intend for me? You speak of my descendants, but you have given me no child. I am an old man now. Some servant of mine will surely inherit this land!"

"No!" said the Lord. "Your own flesh and blood shall inherit it; and this land will belong to your people for all time." Then he took Abraham out into the dark, under the stars. "Look up at the heavens," he said. "Count the stars if you can! That is how many descendants you will have. *For I am the Lord, who brought you* out of Ur; and I shall be your God forever." Then God caused Abraham to see a great vision of a flame and a sacrifice that sealed this promise; and he told him that all men of his tribe must wear from that time on upon their bodies the mark of circumcision. This would be a sign that they, in turn, would keep their covenant with God. Abraham heard and obeyed; and from that day he and his followers were circumcised.

Soon after this, Abraham was sitting by the entrance to his tent in the heat of the day when he suddenly noticed three strangers standing nearby. "My lords," he said to them, "if it please you, come and rest here in the shade and let me refresh you with some cool water and a taste of something to eat." So they came into the shade of the great oak tree beside his tent, and he ran to call Sarah. "Quickly!" he said, "you must knead some loaves for our guests!" He himself took a tender young calf from his herd, and had it prepared for them and brought them also fresh milk and cream. When they had eaten, Abraham looked at his visitors again in wonder, for he saw now that they were angels of the Lord.

"Where is your wife Sarah?" one of the visitors asked. "She is in the tent," Abraham replied. Then the angel said, "I shall visit you again in one year without fail, and by that time you and your wife will have a son." Now, Sarah was listening to all this from inside the tent, and she laughed to herself, thinking, "What an idea! I am too old for any such thing, and so is Abraham! What foolishness is this?"

But the Lord knew what was in her mind, and he said to her, *I am the Lord God! Is anything impossible for me? Why do you laugh, Sarah?* Sarah was afraid. "I did not laugh," she said. But

God replied, "Oh yes, you laughed." And then he went away toward Sodom with the three angels and Abraham.

"There is a great outcry against the people of Sodom and Gomorrah," God said to Abraham. "If they are truly as sinful as I hear, then I am going to destroy this town." Beyond the gates of Sodom he stopped, and Abraham stood before him. "My Lord God," said Abraham, "you are the great judge of all the world. Will you allow good people to be destroyed along with the bad? Suppose there are fifty good men in this place; will you not spare the town because of them?" The Lord replied, "If my servants find fifty just men in Sodom, I will spare the town," and the angels went on ahead and entered the gates.

Abraham said, "I am bold to speak to my God in this way, for I am only a creature made of dust, but suppose there are only forty-five good men in Sodom. Will you spare it, then?" The Lord answered, "If there are forty-five good men there, I will not destroy the town." And Abraham said, "Perhaps there will be only forty, Lord." "I will not do it, then," God said.

After a while Abraham said, "I trust my Lord will not be angry if I ask, but perhaps Sodom has only thirty good men. What then?" "I will spare the town for them," said the Lord. "I am very bold indeed to speak this way," said Abraham. "Forgive me, Lord, but what if there are only twenty good men in Sodom?" God said, "For the sake of the twenty, I will not destroy it." Finally in a very small voice Abraham said, "Do not be angry, Lord, if I speak just once more, but what if there are only ten good men in Sodom?" And the Lord God went away from him then, saying, "If there are ten good men in Sodom, I will not destroy the town."

# The Destruction
# of Sodom

The angels went into Sodom, and there was Lot sitting by the gate. Seeing that they were strangers, he said, "Come to my house and rest; let me serve you." So they did, but the wicked people of the town soon surrounded Lot's house, threatening his visitors. Lot faced the crowd and said, "Leave us in peace! These are my guests! I would sooner let you mistreat my own daughters than harm these men and break God's sacred laws of hospitality!"

The people mocked him and tried to break down the door, but the angels reached out and struck their leaders blind. Then they said to Lot, "Leave this place! Take your family with you! God is angry with these evil people, and he is going to destroy the town. Go into the hills quickly, and do not look back!" Lot could not believe them at first. "But the hills are so far away!" he said. "May I go to the town of Zoar, over there, instead?" The angels replied, "On your account Zoar will be saved—but go!"

So Lot and his family hastened away as the morning sun was rising. Then the rage of heaven came down upon Sodom and Gomorrah; a tremendous earthquake struck, and both towns were utterly destroyed. Lot and his daughters and his sons-in-law were safe; but Lot's wife had turned back for one last glimpse of all she was leaving, and she was changed at that moment into a pillar of salt.

# Abraham and Isaac

The Lord God remembered his promises. When Sarah was ninety and Abraham was one hundred years old, a son was born to them; and they named him Isaac, which means "Laughing One." Sarah laughed now for joy, and Abraham gave a banquet for all his people on the day when the boy was weaned. Throughout his childhood, Isaac was tenderly cared for and very dearly loved.

One day when Isaac was half grown, the Lord put Abraham to the greatest of tests. "Abraham, Abraham," he called to him. "Here I am," Abraham replied. "Take your son," said the Lord, "your only son, Isaac, whom you love so much, and go to the land of Moriah with him. There you shall give him up to me as a burnt offering, in a place on the mountain that I will show you."

Abraham did not close his eyes in sleep that night. Rising up early the next morning, he chopped wood for the fire, and he saddled his donkey, and he awakened his son. Two servants came with them as far as the foot of the mountain, but Abraham told them to wait there, keeping the animals. Then he began to climb the mountain, with Isaac beside him carrying the wood. In his own hands, Abraham carried a torch and a knife for the sacrifice.

"Father?" said Isaac.

"Yes, my son?"

"Look, here are the fire and the wood," said Isaac. "But

where is the lamb for our burnt offering?"

Abraham answered, "My dear son, the Lord God will provide the lamb."

They went on together, and when they came to the place that the Lord had shown Abraham, he stopped and built an altar there. Then he arranged the wood for the sacrificial fire. He bound his son, Isaac, and put him on the altar, above the wood. Finally he reached out his hand for the knife and prepared to kill his son.

At that moment, Abraham heard God calling to him again. "Abraham, Abraham!"

"I am here," he replied.

"Let the boy go," said the Lord. "I do not want you to hurt him. You have shown me today that you refuse me nothing and that you are my true servant in all things. You have been willing to offer up to me the most precious gift I have ever given you: your son, your only son, whose life is dearer to you than your own." Hearing this, Abraham released his son, Isaac, and then they saw a ram caught by its horns in a bush nearby. They took the ram, and Abraham sacrificed it in place of his son.

The Lord God was well pleased. He spoke to Abraham again. "Because of your obedience today," he said, "I will watch over your people forever. Isaac shall live to be the father of many sons and many daughters. The tribe of Abraham shall increase until your descendants are as numerous as the grains of sand upon the seashore; and your enemies shall surrender their towns to you; and all the nations of the earth shall be blessed by the tribe of Abraham."

# Isaac and
# Rebekah

When Isaac was full-grown, Abraham sent his most trusted servant back to their homeland to find him a wife, for he did not want his son to marry among the Canaanites. It was evening when the servant came to the town of Abraham's kin, and he stopped to watch the young women coming one by one to draw water from the well. "O God!" he prayed, "show me the bride you intend for my master's son!"

At that moment, a beautiful maiden came toward him with a

pitcher upon her shoulder. "Drink," she said, "and I will water your camels, too." At this, the servant knew in his heart that she was the one. He went immediately to her parents, carrying gifts of silver and gold from Abraham. "Will you let your daughter come with me to marry my master's son?" he asked. "Let us see what she says," they replied. "Rebekah, do you wish to go?" She said, "I do."

And so Rebekah and the servant traveled back toward Canaan together. Near evening time, the servant saw Isaac walking toward them in the fields. Rebekah gazed at Isaac and jumped down from her camel. "Who is this man?" she cried. The servant smiled. "This is your bridegroom," he told her. Rebekah blushed, and covered her face with her veil. But Isaac greeted her tenderly, and led her into his tent. From that day, Rebekah was Isaac's dearly beloved wife.

# Jacob's Story

When Rebekah was expecting her first child, she felt a great struggle within her, and she cried out to the Lord God in her distress. "You shall have two warring, grappling sons, Rebekah," he answered her, "and the younger shall be master over the elder." Indeed, when her time came to be delivered, Rebekah saw that she had twins. The first to be born was Esau, who had a red and hairy body; after him came Jacob, who was pale and smooth-skinned.

As the boys grew up, Esau roamed the fields and became a mighty hunter. He was his father Isaac's favorite; but Rebekah's heart turned to Jacob, who was a shepherd, a quiet and clever boy who liked to stay with her, among the tents.

One day, Esau came home weary from the hunt and found that Jacob had made a wonderful lentil soup. "Oh, I am starving," said Esau, "give me some of that soup!" Jacob replied, "You may have it if you will give me your birthright." Now, Esau was a rough and simple young man, and he smelled the delicious meal that was in the pot, and thought, "What good will it do me that I was born first if I am dead from hunger?" So he gave Jacob his right, as first born, to lead the family in the future; and he filled his belly full, and thought no more about it.

Meantime, Isaac had become very old and very frail; he knew at last that the hour of his death was upon him. "My son," he said to Esau one morning, "go and hunt some wild venison and make my favorite meal for me once more, so that I may give you my blessing before I die!" Esau went out into the fields, but Rebekah had heard all of this, and she decided to play a trick upon the old man. She wanted the blessing of riches and prosperity for her favorite son, so she dressed Jacob in his brother's clothing. Then she covered his head and arms with the skin of a goat, and sent him to his father's bedside, carrying a splendid stew. "Is that you, Esau?" cried the dying man, who could not see. "Ah, yes, I feel your rough skin, and I smell the beloved fragrance of my firstborn son. I give you my blessing, that you may prosper always—that your kin and all nations may bow down before you, now and forever!"

In this way, Jacob got for himself the blessing meant for his older brother. When Esau discovered what had happened, he was furious. Jacob fled for his life, out of Canaan.

On his journey toward the east, Jacob had a marvelous adventure. Pausing to sleep one night, he used a stone for his pillow as he lay down. Then he dreamed that he saw a ladder standing beside him with its top reaching up to heaven, and with angels going up the ladder and coming down. He heard God say to him, "I am the Lord, the God of Abraham and of your father. I will give you the land where you now lie, and I will make your descendants as many as the specks of dust on the earth around you! Do not fear, for I will be with you always to keep you safe."

Filled with wonder, Jacob rose up early in the morning. "Surely, God himself dwells in this place," he said. And he took the stone that had been his pillow, and he anointed it with oil.

Then he set up the stone as a holy monument, naming that place *Bethel,* which means "House of God."

After this, Jacob traveled to Aram, the land of his kinsman Laban, who was the brother of Rebekah. With tears of joy, he greeted his relatives; and as he stood talking with them in the fields beside their well, he saw a lovely shepherdess drawing near to give water to her sheep. "Here is Rachel, daughter of Laban," his cousins told him. Jacob went to her and kissed her; and from that moment his heart was filled with desire to make her his wife.

"I will work seven years for you if I may marry Rachel," Jacob said to her father, for he had no bridal gifts to offer. "Very well," said Laban, thinking to himself about Rachel's older sister, Leah, who was not nearly so charming as she. So Jacob worked hard, but at the end of the seven years, he was deceived by Laban. Veiled for the marriage feast, Leah was given to him in marriage instead. Now it was Jacob's turn to be furious. "Why have you tricked me?" he asked his father-in-law. "In our country," Laban replied, "the younger sister may not be married before the elder. If you wish to marry Rachel, you must work for me another seven years."

Jacob's love was so great that he did this, and at the end of fourteen years he claimed Rachel as his bride. Still he did not leave Laban's country, but worked there another six years, tending the flocks and gradually collecting a herd of his own. "Go back home now," the Lord said to Jacob after twenty long years, "and remember that I will be with you, wherever you may go." So Jacob set off for the land of Canaan with all his household, and as he went upon his way, he sent rich gifts on ahead to his brother, Esau, hoping to be forgiven at last.

# Jacob Meets an Angel

One night on his journey into Canaan, Jacob lay down to rest by the side of a rushing stream; and a messenger came from God who seized him in a mighty grip and wrestled with him hour after hour, until the light of dawn. Seeing that he could not defeat Jacob, he

struck him upon the hip; and Jacob's hip hurt painfully, but still he would not give in. "Let me go," the angel cried finally, "for day is breaking!" But Jacob answered, "I will not let you go until you have blessed me!"

"What is your name?" the angel asked. "Jacob," he replied. "From this night you shall be called *Israel*," declared the angel. "For that means, '*You have struggled with God and were not defeated.*' " And the angel blessed him and went away. The sun was rising as Jacob crossed the stream, limping, to join the rest of his company. *I have seen the Lord God face to face,* he thought, *and I have survived.*

In a little while he looked out across the plains and saw Esau coming toward him with four hundred men. He went ahead of his household and bowed low to the ground seven times before approaching his brother. "I come to you," Jacob said, "trembling as in the presence of God." But Esau's heart went out to him, and he took Jacob up in his arms and embraced him and wept for joy. From that time on, the brothers helped one another and remained at peace.

# Joseph and His Brothers

This is the story of Joseph.

The son of Jacob and Rachel was a shepherd named Joseph; and he was a dreamer of many dreams. When Joseph was very young, he told his brothers, "I dreamed that I saw your sheaves of grain gathered in a circle, bowing down before mine." His brothers were not pleased to hear this. Later Joseph told them, "I dreamed that I saw the sun, the moon, and the stars bow down before me!" and at this, his brothers became angry indeed. Joseph's father, Jacob (who was now known as *Israel*) also rebuked him, but in time it was easy to see that he loved Joseph more than his other sons. He had a fine coat made for Joseph—a coat of many colors, with long sleeves, like the garment of a prince; and this coat finally made Joseph's brothers half mad with jealousy.

"Go out into the fields and find your brothers," Israel said to Joseph one day. "Then come and tell me how they are and whether my flocks are doing well." So Joseph set off into the countryside, and his brothers saw him coming a long way off.

"Here comes the man of dreams," said Joseph's brothers. "Come, let us lay hands on him and kill him. We can tell our father that a wild beast has devoured him; and that will be an end of this princeling with his boasting and his fancy coat."

But one of Joseph's brothers, whose name was Reuben, intended to save him; so he said, "Do not take his life! Only put him down into this dry well, and leave him here!" Joseph approached, and his brothers seized him and stripped off his coat. Then they threw him down into the well, and they themselves sat down to eat.

As they were finishing their meal, the brothers looked up and saw a band of Ishmaelite merchants going by with their camels laden. This gave them an idea. "Let us not do any more harm to Joseph," said his brother Judah. "After all, he is our brother, and our flesh and blood! Let us merely sell him into slavery."

So they went to find Joseph in the well, but as it happened, he had already been stolen away by another band of travelers and brought to the Ishmaelites. Reuben saw him gone and cried out in fear, "What shall we do?" The other brothers gathered together then, plotting a way to hide their wickedness from their father, Israel. They killed a goat and smeared its blood upon Joseph's fine coat; then they sent the bloodstained garment back to their father with a message, asking him, "Is this the clothing of your son?"

"Alas, alas, it is," cried Israel. "My son is dead! He must have been torn to pieces and devoured by some wild beast, for see— here is his blood!" And Joseph's father wept, and he put on mourning clothes of sackcloth for his son, and would not be comforted. But Joseph, meantime, had been sold to the Ishmaelites for twenty pieces of silver. He was alive, a slave among camels laden with gum and resin, bound for the land of Egypt.

# Joseph

Joseph was sold into slavery; yet all was not lost, for the Lord God was with him as he was carried away into that rich and fertile land by the banks of the river Nile. There Joseph was bought by a man named Potiphar, who was commander of the Pharaoh's guards. Immediately after this, Potiphar noticed that things began going unusually well for him. He did not know that this was because the spirit of God was with Joseph, but he was delighted with his new slave. Soon he put Joseph in charge of all that he owned, and of his entire household.

Now, Joseph was an extremely good-looking young man,

and the wife of Potiphar took a fancy to him. "Come here and pay attention to me," she begged him time after time when her husband was away. But Joseph was loyal to his master, and he would not. Still she pursued him, for this lady was used to having her own way; yet he always managed to escape her, and finally Potiphar's wife was in a towering rage. "That miserable slave of

yours has tried to make love to me!" she cried to her husband one day. "He must be punished!" Unfortunately Potiphar believed her, and so Joseph was thrown into prison for a crime of which he was innocent. Once in prison, he was entirely forgotten by his master and his former friends.

Yet even now all was not lost, for God watched over Joseph in the very depths of the prison where he lay for two long years. With the Lord's help, Joseph interpreted the dreams of his fellow prisoners; and he became their favorite companion and the favorite also of the prison guards. At last, word reached the ears of the Pharaoh himself that a splendid young man had been imprisoned—a person who understood the meaning of dreams. "Bring the young Hebrew slave to me," said Pharaoh. "I wish to consult him." So the jailers set Joseph free, and in clean, new garments he was led into the court.

"Tell me," said the monarch of Egypt, "what I should think of this dream. I saw coming up from the River Nile seven fine cows all sleek and fat. Then seven thin cows came after them, and devoured them all. After that I dreamed of seven fine ears of corn that were eaten before my eyes by seven bad ears."

"The meaning of this is clear," Joseph said immediately. "The land of Egypt is rich now, and the crops are good; none of Your Lordship's subjects hungers for food. Yet it will not always be so. After seven years of plenty, there will be seven lean years ahead, and we must store up food against that time of distress. What you need, O Pharaoh, is a knowledgeable person to go among your people and see that they put supplies away now, in a safe place. Then your people will not suffer famine, later on."

"I believe that you are right," said the Pharaoh. "Furthermore, I see that the leader we need to do this job is standing before me." And so, at that very moment, he put Joseph in charge of the wealth of Egypt. He gave him power to tax the people and to have huge stores of foodstuffs put aside from their harvests so that they would be available when needed. Joseph the prisoner was now governor of all the land, and he did his work so well that people from all over the world came to Egypt to buy food when the time of famine came.

For the time did come, and this is how it happened that Joseph's brothers appeared at the court one day, seeking to buy food for their hungry families back in Canaan. Ten of them arrived together, but the youngest, Benjamin (who was his father's chief joy in the absence of Joseph), was left behind for safety's sake. In the court of the Pharaoh, Joseph's brothers stood before him and did not recognize him; they saw only a powerful Egyptian governor. Humbly they begged him to let them buy food.

Joseph treated them harshly at first. "You are spies," he said to them. "I will sell you no food until your youngest brother, Benjamin, is brought to me." Hearing this, the brother named Reuben told the others in their own language, "You see, I told you not to harm Joseph. Now in our time of trouble, we are made to pay for that old sin of ours!" Reuben did not know that Joseph could understand this, and he did not see Joseph turning his face away hastily, to hide his tears.

Back to Canaan the brothers traveled, deeply discouraged, and when they arrived they wondered how it was that their saddlebags had been mysteriously filled with money and with food. "The governor of Egypt asked many questions about you," they told their old father. "We do not understand that! It was all very strange!" Their father replied, "I only know that I lost my beloved Joseph, and now I must lose Benjamin, too. I do not know how I will bear it," and he bowed his head with grief. Yet they had no choice. Food was so badly needed that they decided they must obey the governor.

Once more to Egypt the brothers came, bringing young Benjamin with them this time. When Joseph saw them returning, he had a great feast prepared for them, and he gave them many rich gifts, still without telling them his real name. Then he asked once more about the health of his old father. "He is in despair," the brothers replied. "He knows that you mean to keep Benjamin here as a slave; but he has suffered so much already from the loss of another son that he will surely die of grief if you do not return the boy."

At this, Joseph could contain himself no longer. He burst into tears and rushed from the room. When he returned, after bathing his face, he said to them, "I am Joseph, your brother, whom you sold into Egypt," and he embraced them all with many fresh tears. "Do not grieve," he told them. "All of this was done by God, so that I might prepare a way for you to be fed in the time of famine."

He sent his brothers back into Canaan then, telling them to collect all the descendants of Israel and to bring them quickly into Egypt. Here he promised that they would be given all the food they could eat and a safe pasturage for their flocks. Then Joseph had his chariot made ready, and he went out to meet his aged father. In the land of Goshen, by the Egyptian border, they caught sight of one another, and Joseph's father embraced him, weeping with joy. "Now I can die in peace," he said, "for I have seen my son Joseph once again, and I know that he is alive and well!"

But Israel did not die for many years. He lived to bless all of his sons and all of their people; and the tribes of Israel continued to grow and prosper as peace-loving shepherds in the land of plenty that the Lord had provided for them.

# Moses

After the death of Joseph, a new Pharaoh came to the throne; and he noticed that the tribe of Israel was very large by now and very strong. "We must do something about these people," he thought, "or they will overpower us." So he forced the Israelites to do slave labor and made their lives nearly unbearable with heavy work; yet even then he was not satisfied. "All of their boy children must be drowned in the Nile from now on," the Pharaoh declared. "That

will soon be the end of these upstart foreigners!"

At about this time, an Israelite woman gave birth to a fine baby boy, and she hid him away so that he would not be put to death. When she could no longer conceal him, she carried her little son to the river Nile and put him into a basket that she had prepared very carefully, so that it would float. Weeping, she placed the basket among the reeds and waited nearby, in secret.

In a little while the Pharaoh's daughter came to the river to bathe, with all her handmaidens attending her. "Listen!" the princess said. "There is a baby crying!" And she found the child and took him up in her arms. "I shall keep this baby," said the Pharaoh's daughter, "and his name shall be *Moses*." Thus it was that Moses was saved to become in time the champion of his people; and thus he was raised as a prince in the court of his enemies.

# Moses and the God of Abraham

**M**oses was troubled and angry as he grew up, seeing the cruel mistreatment of his people in Egypt. What could he do to help them? He did not know. One day as the young man was tending his flocks in the wilderness, he looked up toward Mount Sinai, which is called the mountain of God. There on the path before him was a flame of fire that seemed to be coming from a burning bush; and the bush continued to burn, yet it was not consumed. "Moses, Moses!" called the voice of the Lord from the center of the flame. "Here I am," answered Moses; but he covered his face, for he was afraid to look at God. "Who is it who calls me?" he asked.

"I am the God of your fathers," said the Lord. "*I am who I am.* I have been the God of Abraham and of Isaac and of Jacob before you; and I have seen the suffering of my people, the people of Israel, who are my firstborn sons. I mean for you to deliver them from their slave masters, and lead them out of Egypt into a land that is rich and free, a land where milk and honey flow. You must go to the Pharaoh now, and say to him, 'The God of the Hebrews has come to meet us. Therefore let his people go for three days into the wilderness, so that we may worship him and offer him sacrifice.' "

"How can I do such a thing?" asked Moses. "He will pay no attention to me! All my life I have been a slow speaker and very awkward with words."

58

"Who gave you a mouth? Who gave you speech to speak with?" answered the Lord. "Do not argue with me. Go to the Pharaoh and I shall help you, and I shall tell you what to say to him. If marvels are needed to persuade him, I shall give you power to show this Pharaoh many strange signs."

So Moses went, together with his brother Aaron, before the Pharaoh and told him, "The God of Israel has come to meet us. He wants us to come out into the wilderness, and he tells you, *Let my people go!*"

"Who is this God of the Hebrews?" Pharaoh replied. "Why should I listen to him? I will not let them go!"

Then the Lord spoke to Moses again. "Throw your staff down before the Pharaoh," he said. So Moses did, and his staff was turned into a mighty serpent, on the spot. The Pharaoh and his court were amazed, but they still refused the request of Moses; and the Pharaoh issued orders that the people of Israel must work harder than ever from now on.

"This Pharaoh has a stubborn heart," said God. "He must be visited with plagues, it seems, before he will obey." And so the Lord sent down nine plagues upon the land of Egypt, one after another, to show his power. "Raise your hands," he said to Moses, "and strike the waters of the river with your staff." Moses did, and the first plague struck the river—a plague that turned all the waters of Egypt into blood. Still the Pharaoh would not relent. There followed a plague of frogs and a plague of gnats; then a plague of flies and a plague of illness that killed the livestock of the Egyptians far and wide. But the Pharaoh would not let God's people go. Next there was a plague of boils, then one of hail; then a plague of locusts that devoured the countryside. The ninth plague Moses brought upon Egypt with his power from God was a plague of darkness, and by now the Pharaoh was badly frightened. Still he would not let the Israelites go; he wanted them to continue working as his slaves. He said to Moses only, "Get out of my sight! Never appear in this court again or you will die!"

"You have said it," replied Moses. "I shall, indeed, go away."

Then the Lord told Moses, "One more lesson for the Pharaoh remains, and then you will be set free. Listen carefully now, for I speak to you of the feast of the Passover, which shall be celebrated by the people of Israel from now on until the end of time." Then God told Moses that all Israelites must prepare unleavened bread and eat no other kind for seven days, in preparation for their flight. Also they must sacrifice a lamb from every household, and each must mark his own doorposts with the blood of this animal. "At midnight I shall pass over Egypt," said the Lord. "In every unmarked house, the firstborn of that family shall die. Only the Children of Israel shall be spared, and there shall be wailing throughout the land. But they shall see that I favor you, for *I am the Lord God*, and at last they shall let you go."

The people of Israel did exactly as God instructed them, and soon they were ready for the great journey to come. But before the day of the tenth plague, the Lord gathered their elders together and said to them, "Keep the rules of the Passover always, and obey them every year! When your children ask you, 'What is the meaning of this ritual?' tell them it is a sacrifice for the Lord—that it is done in remembrance of the God who came to meet them, and who brought them out of bondage into the Promised Land."

# Crossing the Sea

When the people of Egypt found their own firstborn children killed and those of Israel safe, after the night of the first Passover, a terrible cry went up throughout the land. The Israelites fled for their lives. They went fully armed, taking with them only what they could carry, and their bread, which, in their haste, was still unleavened. On the shore of the Sea of Reeds (often called the Red Sea), they made camp before crossing into the wilderness beyond.

Meantime the Pharaoh thought to himself, "These people were good workers. We should not have let them go!" And he gathered up all his troops and came after them. The Israelites saw that tremendous horde approaching, and they were terrified. "Were there no graves in Egypt?" they asked Moses. "Did you have to bring us out here to die instead?"

"Be calm," Moses told them, "the Lord will fight for us." Then he raised his staff, and God sent a great wind before it to force the waters aside. The Israelites made their crossing quickly then, on dry land. The Pharaoh tried to follow them, but just at this moment, God made the waters come flooding back. The children of Israel stood on the opposite shore, watching and wondering; before their eyes, the vast army of the Egyptian monarch was destroyed—and all his men were drowned, and all his horses went down, and all his armor, and his banners, and his swift and mighty chariots.

# The Cloud

**W**hen Moses and the Children of Israel saw the Pharaoh's army destroyed, they lifted their voices in song:

> *The Lord is my strength and my protection!*
> *The Lord will be king forever!*
> *Sing of the Lord, he has covered himself in glory:*
> *Horse and rider he has thrown into the sea.*

So they sang, and Miriam the Prophetess took up her timbrel and danced, and all the women followed her. In a mood of jubilation

# nd the Fire

the Israelites began their journey into the desert, toward the land of Canaan, which lay beyond. They thought that they would come very soon into the place of milk and honey and rich, green pastures. But God had other plans for them; he knew that they had much to learn before they would be ready to take possession of the Promised Land.

After a few days in the desert, the Israelites were very thirsty and very hungry and quite discouraged. After a few weeks, they had begun to complain bitterly to Moses. "We had plenty of meat

and bread in Egypt," they said, "and plenty of good water to drink. Why ever did you want us to leave? You have brought us out here to starve us to death in the wilderness!" Moses went to the Lord and asked, "What am I to do with these people? They are losing their faith in you, and if this goes on, they may do me violence!"

"Go to the Rock of Horeb," God replied, "and I shall go there before you. When you strike that rock with your staff, water will flow from it." Moses obeyed. The power of the Lord made water spring from the rock for the people to drink, and they were glad of this; yet soon they were grumbling again, for they were hungry and there was very little to eat. "Is God with us or not?" they cried to Moses. *How stubborn these people are!* Moses thought.

Soon after this, the Israelites looked up at the sky one day and they saw the glory of the Lord appearing to them in the form of a great cloud. "I shall rain down bread from heaven upon you," God said to Moses from the cloud. "You shall find it in the morning; and for six days the people may gather it. But on the seventh day they must not, for that is the sabbath, which is holy to me. Let us see whether these greedy people will obey me!"

And in the morning, when the dew had lifted, the Israelites found upon the desert something delicate and white that tasted like wafers made of honey and coriander seed. They called it manna, and they found that it was delicious to eat. At first they did go out to look for it on the seventh day, despite God's rule, but it never appeared then; and so they learned to keep the sabbath, as he had intended. For forty years, the Children of Israel were nourished by this food that came from God in the wilderness.

In time, they came to the land of Sinai, and there at the foot of the mountain they pitched their tents, seeing that there was a great cloud upon the mountaintop and that, within the cloud, there was a fire. "Prepare the people," the Lord said to Moses, "for it is time for me to speak with you once more. On eagles' wings I have brought you out of Egypt, for of all nations you are my very own. Now I will make a covenant with you. I intend to make you into a nation of priests and a holy people; be ready now to hear my laws!" The people washed themselves and waited quietly at the foot of the mountain, but they were terrified. "Speak to God for us," they begged Moses. "We see his cloud and his fire! If we see him face to face, then we will surely die!"

On the third day after this there was thunder on Mount Sinai, and the sound of a mighty trumpet was heard. The earth shook, and a pillar of flame appeared on high. Moses went up the mountain, and there, from the very heart of the fire, God spoke to him. *These are my Commandments*, he said:

*I am the Lord God who brought you out of Egypt, out of slavery.*

*You must have no other gods but me. You must not make a likeness of anything on earth and worship it, for I am a jealous God.*

*My name is holy. You must not use it lightly or use it in the making of false vows.*

*Remember the sabbath day. Rest from your labors and honor me on this day.*

*Honor your father and your mother.*

*You must not kill.*

*Marriage is sacred; you must not commit adultery.*

You must not steal.
You must not tell lies about the doings of another person.
You must not set your heart on having another man's wife,
or on owning anything that belongs to him.

So that they would remember them always, God carved the Ten Commandments upon tablets of stone for the Children of Israel; and Moses stayed on the mountain for forty days and forty nights.

# The Golden Calf

When Moses came down from the mountain, his face was shining so brightly with the glory of God that the people were afraid to look at him. But they had another reason, too, to be afraid. During his long absence, they had forgotten the love of God, and with Aaron's help they had set up a golden calf to worship instead. Moses found them dancing and singing the praises of this bestial image, and his heart was hot with rage. He took the tablets of the law that the Lord had given him and broke them at the foot of the mountain; and he burned the golden calf and ground it to powder; and he cast the powder into the people's drinking water.

Aaron said to Moses, "Do not be so angry! You know these Israelites. They are always doing wicked things. They did not know what had happened to you, and they wanted some god to help them through the wilderness. So they put the gold into the fire, and somehow it turned itself into a calf!"

But Moses was furious. He said to Aaron and the Israelites, "You have sinned miserably, you foolish people. I must go up again now to the Lord and see whether he will forgive you for my sake." Up to the top of Mount Sinai Moses went once more then, weary and discouraged, to speak face to face with God, as a man speaks to his friend.

**M**oses went up the mountain again, carrying fresh tablets of stone to receive the word of the Lord, and God descended in a cloud to meet him there. Moses bowed down his head and worshiped him. "O Lord," he said, "I know this is a stiff-necked people. Still, if I have found favor in your sight, I pray you to forgive us all and stay with us on our journey through the wilderness!"

The glory of the Lord shone bright around him, and the Lord said, "I am God and I am a merciful God, gracious and slow to anger, and filled with a steadfast love. Yet those who have sinned shall suffer for it, and their sins shall be visited upon the generations. Behold! I will make a covenant with you today. Obey

me and you shall see the work that God will do for Israel. Other nations will be driven before you and you shall possess the land of Canaan. You shall break down the altars of the Canaanites and destroy the idols of all other peoples who worship false gods! You shall win a great and terrible victory, if only you are faithful to me. Now, write down my laws once more, and keep them as I intend!" So Moses wrote down the Ten Commandments again, and brought them to his people.

Those who had worshiped the golden calf were punished by a plague, and there was war among the Israelites, between the faithful and the unfaithful. Brother was slain by brother, and a time of mourning followed, when the guilty were filled with remorse

and all the Israelites were fearful about the future. But Moses pitched a tent at some distance, and he called it the *tent of meeting*. Whenever he entered this tent, the people rose to their feet and bowed their heads, for a pillar of cloud would descend upon it, and there within the thick darkness of the cloud, Moses would speak with God. "Show me your ways, O Lord," Moses prayed. "Help me to teach your people what to do, so that you will stay with us always."

In the tent of meeting, the Lord God taught Moses many things. In order to worship him rightly, the Lord said, the Israelites must make a holy tabernacle for him, and an ark within the tabernacle to contain the writings of his laws. "Take from among you offerings for the Lord," he told them. "Take gold and silver and bronze, take blue and purple and scarlet cloth, and fine linen, and take acacia wood. Take onyx stones and spices, and incense and oils. Use these things in the building of my tabernacle, but do not work on the seventh day, for that is the sabbath, which is sacred to me."

So the Children of Israel brought their precious wood and cloth and gems, and began to build the tabernacle according to the directions that God gave to Moses. First they made curtains of blue and purple and scarlet cloth, with cherubim skillfully worked in; and each curtain was forty-two feet long and six feet wide. The curtains were set upon a frame of acacia wood, and they were looped with blue and clasped with clasps of gold, so as to make a hidden, holy space inside. The tabernacle was covered then with a tent made of goatskin, and fine silver was used for its base, and bronze was used for the base of the tent.

A veil was made to cover the entrance to the sanctuary, and within it they placed an ark of acacia wood overlaid with pure gold, with a ring of gold at each corner and poles of wood to go through the rings so that the ark containing God's laws could be carried with them wherever they might go. In this space, above the ark, they made a mercy seat of gold, and two cherubim overshadowing it with golden wings. And beyond the veil, in the court of the tabernacle, they placed a table made of acacia wood with golden rings and wooden poles to carry it; and on the table, vessels of gold, and a lampstand made of gold with three branches on either side and seven golden lamps.

Here in the court they also placed the holy altar with its vessels for incense and burnt offerings; and then God told Moses, "You shall bring Aaron and his sons to the door of the tent, and you shall wash and anoint them, and dress them in priestly garments, so that they and their descendants shall serve me as priests, throughout the generations."

When all of this had been done according to God's word, the cloud descended to cover the holy tent, and the glory of the Lord filled the tabernacle so brightly that even Moses was not able, at first, to enter it. From that time on, the Israelites carried the Ark of the Covenant with them everywhere they went. When they saw that the cloud of God's presence had descended upon the tabernacle, and covered it over entirely, they did not continue on their journey, but waited until it should move away. And throughout all their wanderings in the wilderness in days to come, the Children of Israel knew that God was with them, for they could see above their tabernacle his pillar of cloud by day and his pillar of fire by night.

# Love and Law

Before the Israelites left Sinai, Moses met God within the tabernacle many times. "Speak to the people of Israel again," said the Lord. "Teach them more of my laws. My love for them has made them a holy nation; I want to show them how to be cleansed of all their sins."

So God taught Moses, and Moses taught the people. First they learned the rules for making offerings to God, whether of grain or of creatures from their flocks. They learned to make these sacrifices sometimes for thanking and praising God, and at other times to show him that they were sorry for something wicked they had done. They learned exactly what their priests should do to keep them holy so that all should receive God's mercy.

Then God taught the people which living creatures were considered clean, and therefore pure and pleasing in his sight; and they learned which were considered unclean. There were many special laws of health and cleanliness for the Children of Israel to obey; and there were days that must be set aside for certain purposes every year. One of these was the day of the Passover, when the Lord had brought them out of Egypt. Another was the Day of Atonement, which he wanted them to celebrate as the most solemn sabbath of all. On the Day of Atonement, two goats should be chosen out of their flocks, and one was to be sacrificed as a burnt offering for the sins of the whole nation. The other was to be driven away, bearing with it into the desert wastes all of the people's wickedness.

"Hear, O Israel," the Lord said to Moses, "I am the Lord, your only God. In days to come you will meet many pagan people. You will be tempted to worship with them and to obey their laws instead of mine. Be strong! Guard your families and show respect to every member of this nation! Beware the wizards and magicians you will meet, and beware especially the evil Molech, god of the Canaanites: Do not sacrifice your children to him!

"Do not please yourselves," said the Lord, "at the expense of your family members or your neighbors. If one of you harms another, you must see to it that he is punished, an eye for an eye, a tooth for a tooth. It is my law that you must love your neighbor as yourself! And you shall cherish also the stranger and the sojourner, for you were strangers in the land of Egypt!"

Then God told Moses to count all the members of the twelve tribes of Israel, and list them all in a census, before beginning the next part of their journey; there were many thousands of Israelites by now. Moses and Aaron were members of the Levite tribe; and God taught them that the Levites should be set aside from the others as the chief priests of Israel throughout the generations. "Thus shall you bless my people," God said to the Levites. "Thus shall you place my name upon them, and say to them,

> *The Lord bless you and keep you,*
> *The Lord make his face to shine upon you*
> *and be gracious unto you:*
> *The Lord lift up his countenance upon you*
> *and give you peace."*

# Journeying toward Canaan

The cloud was taken up from the tabernacle, and the hosts of Israel set out toward the land of Canaan, carrying the Ark of the Lord before them. It was a hard journey, and the people very soon began to complain once more. "We are thirsty," they said to Moses, "and we are hungry! We have nothing but this manna from God now to sustain us; but we remember the fish we ate in Egypt, and we remember the cucumbers, and the melons, and leeks! How shall we survive in this terrible place?" Moses prayed to the Lord again, asking, "What am I meant to do about these people? I did not give birth to them! I cannot suckle them and carry them about like babies—the burden is too heavy for me!"

"Choose seventy among the elders," God told Moses. "I will put some of my spirit into them, so that they may help you." At this, a young warrior named Joshua came to Moses and said, "Eldad and Medad are prophesying in the camp. My lord Moses, forbid them!" But Moses said to him, "Are you jealous for my sake? Would that all the Lord's people were prophets with the spirit of the Lord upon them!" And they continued on their way.

At the oasis of Kadesh the Israelites made camp, and there they stayed for a time, preparing themselves for an attack upon Canaan from the south. Spies were sent into the Promised Land, and when they returned their eyes were wide with wonder. They

brought with them figs and pomegranates for the people, and a single bunch of grapes so huge that it had to be carried on poles between two men. "It is a rich and gracious country, and it will be easy for us to capture," said Joshua and Caleb. "We saw Anakites, Amalekites and Hittites there. We saw Jebusites and Amorites; and there are Canaanites living by the river Jordan and by the sea. But let us go bravely now and take possession of it all, for God is with us and he has promised it to us!"

But some of the men who had gone with Caleb and Joshua were frightened. "These people are powerful," they reported. "The Anakites are giants, compared to us!" Then the Israelites cried out in terror, saying to one another, "Let us go back to Egypt! We have had enough of this Moses and his prophecies! We have suffered in the desert for years—must we die now by the sword?" They decided at last to attack Canaan from the south, but their love of God had lapsed; they failed to bring the Ark of the Covenant with them into battle, and the spirit of the Lord was not with them.

"How long will these people despise me?" said the Lord. "They have seen my signs and wonders, yet they are cowards and unbelievers still. Very well, they shall die in the desert. It shall be their children who shall enter into their inheritance."

And so it was that the Israelites spent forty years in all, in the wilderness. The Amalekites and the Canaanites came down out of the hills and utterly defeated them, driving them back into the wilderness of Zin. Aaron died, and Miriam the Prophetess died; and the Children of Israel wandered still, east toward Moab, trying to find a way to enter the Promised Land.

# The Story of
# Balaam the Magician

Out of the wilderness the Israelites came at last into the land of the Amorites, east of the river Jordan and north of the Salt Sea. The people there would not let the Children of Israel pass through peacefully, and so they fought a number of bloody battles, taking possession of the Amorite settlements and even of Heshbon, the city of the King. The King was slain, and all his sons; and when the Israelites then moved on to the plains of Moab, pitching their tents across from Jericho, the people of Moab trembled with fear. "Behold," said the king of Moab, "a people has come out of Egypt and they cover the face of the earth! As the ox devours the grasses of the fields, surely they will destroy us all!"

So Balak the king of Moab sent his elders to a powerful magician he knew, a man named Balaam, who lived in the mountains of the east. "Come here," he told the wizard, "and place a curse upon these Israelites so that I may be able to drive them away!"

"Lodge here tonight," Balaam said to the messengers. "I must ask the Lord for advice about this." Then Balaam slept, and the Lord God came to him in a dream. "You shall not go to Moab," said the Lord, "and you shall not put a curse upon these people, for they are blessed!" In the morning, Balaam told the elders of Moab what had happened, and they went back to Balak without him.

Next, the King sent princes of his realm to Balaam, promising that he should be richly rewarded if he should obey. "Though he gave me a house full of silver and gold," replied Balaam, "I would

obey only my Lord God." Nevertheless, he decided to go to Moab, and he rose up in the morning and saddled his ass.

As they trotted along the road, the ass looked up and saw the angel of the Lord standing in his way with a drawn sword. The ass turned aside into a field, and this annoyed Balaam so that he struck her with his staff. Then, in a path between walls in the vineyards, the angel of the Lord appeared again. The ass swerved aside, pressing Balaam's foot against the wall, and he struck her once more. Now the angel went on ahead and waited in a space so narrow that there was no room to pass. The ass lay down under Balaam and refused to budge. The magician was furious! He struck the animal for the third time, and at this, the Lord opened the mouth of the ass and let her speak. "Why do you treat me this way?" she asked. "I am your own faithful creature who has carried you all your life. Have I ever behaved in such a way before?" And Balaam replied, "No, you have not."

Then the Lord opened his eyes so that he also saw the angel. Balaam bowed low and begged for mercy. "Go to the king of Moab," said the angel, "but tell him only what I bid you to say!" So Balaam went to the king, and this is what he told him:

> It is God who brings these people out of Egypt!
> How can I curse a people he has blessed?
> No enchantment can destroy this nation,
> For they will devour all who stand against them!
> Behold, O Israel, how fair are your tents,
> Like gardens, like cedar trees that the Lord has planted.
> Blessed be everyone who blesses you,
> For your star shall rise, and your dwellings shall endure.

# The Farewell
# of Moses

When the Israelites made camp near the river Jordan across from Jericho, Moses was a very old man, although he was still strong and his eye was still bright. One day, God spoke to him and said, "Behold, the day is coming when you must die and be gathered to sleep with your forefathers. Therefore, bring Joshua to the tent of meeting, for he has my spirit in him. Lay your hands upon him in the sight of all the people; for it is Joshua who will conquer Canaan and lead the nation into the Promised Land."

So Moses summoned Joshua and did as God commanded. "Be strong and courageous," he told the young warrior. "The Lord will be with you and he will not fail you or forsake you." Then Moses said to the Lord, "Is it true, then, that I will never set foot in Canaan? Let me go over, I pray you, and see that good land beyond the Jordan. Let me see that sweet hill country, and Lebanon." But the Lord denied him, because the Israelites under his care had turned away from their faith at Kadesh, in the wilderness.

Then Moses began to think about all the long years of struggle and hardship he had known. His heart was heavy, and he was troubled, knowing that his people would soon move on without him, into a new life. Would they remember all that he had taught them? Would they obey the laws that God had decreed for a holy people? He knew that they would not—that they would be prideful and foolish, hankering after the false gods of new lands.

In the days that followed, Moses spoke to the Israelites many times. He reminded them of all that had happened to them over the years, and he taught them all he could that might serve to strengthen them against the future. "I am one hundred and twenty years old," he said to them, "and I remember how we came out of Egypt into the desert. At Sinai we saw the cloud of God and his pillar of smoke. And you came near and you stood at the foot of the mountain while the heart of heaven burned. What other nation has been so near to God? What people on earth have received laws that are so righteous and so just?"

"Do not forget," said Moses, "that he spoke to you out of the fire. Obey him always! He has promised you a land flowing with milk and honey; but the Lord our God is a jealous God. Beware his anger and his punishment! He can wipe you from the face of the earth! When you have come into Canaan, you must destroy the places where other nations have worshiped, upon the mountains and under the green trees. Tear down their altars, hew down the images of their gods. But search always for the place that our Lord God shall show you, where he alone will dwell, and there bring your holy offerings."

And Moses taught the people many other things, explaining to them the ceremonies they must keep, and the attitudes they must show to the world at all times, and the rules of behavior that they must obey. "When you go forth to war against your enemies," he said, "do not tremble if their numbers are greater

than yours! Have no fear of their horses and their chariots. The God of Israel will fight for you! Bring into battle only the bravest of your men; and you shall see the cities of your enemies burned before your eyes as a tribute to God."

Then Moses blessed the people and told them this great commandment: *"Hear, O Israel: The Lord our God is one God; and you shall love the Lord your God with all your heart, and with all your soul, and with all your might!"* And Moses said, "Hold these words in your hearts. Write them down where they may be seen, and teach them always, without fail, to your children. Man does not live by bread alone, but by every word that comes from God. He offers you life or death—death which is wickedness, or life which is love of him and obedience to his word. Therefore, choose life!"

The day had come at last for Moses to be gathered to rest with Abraham and Isaac. And the Lord God took him up to a high mountain where he could stand and look out as far as the Sea of Galilee on the north, and on the south to the wilderness of Negeb. He could see across the land of Canaan to the west as far as the great Mediterranean, and below him on the plain he could see the valley of the Jordan and the city of Jericho, green with palms. "This is the land I have promised to Abraham and his descendants. You may not go there, but I have let you see it this day with your own eyes," said the Lord.

For a long time, Moses gazed upon the land: the long green valleys rich with fruit, the rolling river he would never cross, the cities shining in the sun. Then, far from the eyes of any man, he died; and God himself buried Moses in a place so secret that no one has found it to this day.

# Joshua and the Conquest of Canaan

After the death of Moses, the Lord came to Joshua and said, "Moses my servant is dead; therefore you and all the people must go now across the river and into the land that I am giving to Israel. You shall win it for your own wherever your foot shall tread, from the wilderness to the northern mountains of Lebanon, and from here to the realm in the west, where the sun goes down over the sea." So Joshua commanded the people to make ready for battle; and then he sent two men secretly across the river Jordan into Jericho, as spies. They came to the house of a woman of the town called Rahab; but the King of Jericho heard about them, and sent his soldiers to capture them.

"Some men were here, but they have left already," Rahab told the King's men. "If you hurry, you may catch up with them!" And the soldiers went away, but Rahab had hidden the Israelites on the roof of her house, under a pile of flax. She crept up to her roof in the dark and told the spies, "I know the Lord has given you this land! Everyone here knows it! Your God is Lord of heaven and earth, and we are terrified. No one wants to fight against you! Now that I have saved you, will you swear by the God of Israel that you will not harm me or my family?"

"Bind this scarlet cord to your window," said the spies. "Stay

here when the city falls, and we swear that you will be safe."
Rahab let them down from her window by night, and they
returned to their camp, rejoicing. "They are afraid of us," they told
Joshua. "The city is ours!"

The next day, the Israelites began to cross the Jordan, and as
soon as the priests carrying the Ark had put their feet into the
water, the river stopped flowing so that they were able to cross
easily; and all the people followed them. At this, the Lord said,
"Take twelve stones and place them in the river here. When your
children ask you in years to come what these stones mean, tell
them that the Lord of Israel cut off the waters for the Ark of the
Covenant." Then he told Joshua that the people must be cleansed
and that all Israelite men born in the desert must be circumcised.

The people obeyed, and they celebrated the Passover camped near Gilgal, on the plains of Jericho. They ate the unleavened bread of Canaan now, and from this time on the Lord sent no more manna to them.

A short time after this, Joshua stood before the walls of Jericho, looking up at the city with its great buildings of stone and its palms tossing in the wind, beyond the gates. The gates were shut and no one went in or out; but he suddenly saw a man standing before him, with a drawn sword. "Are you for us?" asked Joshua, "or are you for our enemies?" The man said, "I am commander of the army of the Lord God!" And Joshua fell down upon the ground and worshiped him. The angel of the Lord told Joshua how to capture the city, and Joshua told the people

everything he had said. "Do exactly as I have commanded," he warned the Israelites. "Do not harm the house of Rahab and take nothing that the Lord intends to destroy, for the city is to be taken as a tribute to him alone. Save only the vessels of gold and silver, iron and bronze that are sacred to God."

So the fighting men of Israel marched around Jericho once each day for six days, with seven priests sounding seven trumpets as they carried the Ark. On the seventh day they marched around the city seven times. Then, at a long blast of the trumpets, the Israelites gave a tremendous shout; and the walls of Jericho fell down before their eyes. The warriors rushed into the city and utterly destroyed it. All of the people were put to death; they saved only the sacred vessels from the smoldering ruins, and they brought Rahab and her family safely out. "Cursed be he who rebuilds Jericho," said Joshua. "We destroyed it in obedience to God!"

Thus the Israelites began their fierce and bloody conquest of the Promised Land. Many more cities were to fall before them, and many more violent battles were to be fought. During the time that followed, the Lord God of Israel continued to work his signs and wonders for them; and he also taught them that they would be punished if they did not obey his laws.

Soon after the fall of Jericho, the Israelites attacked the settlement of Ai, east of Bethel, and there they were badly defeated. Joshua cried out in anguish, "Alas, my God, why have you brought us to this place? What is to become of us, and what will happen to your great name as the Lord of Battle?"

"Israel has sinned," replied the Lord. "One of your men is a thief, and he has lied! He stole from Jericho things that I had marked for destruction. He must pay the penalty!"

Indeed, Joshua discovered that a man named Achan had

taken a splendid mantle from Jericho, and two hundred shekels of silver, and a talent of gold for himself. When the people realized that God was punishing them all for this, they stoned Achan to death and the things he had stolen were destroyed. When they had been cleansed of this sin, the Israelites easily took possession of Ai.

Later in the campaign, the five Amorite kings banded together in a mighty effort to defeat Joshua's forces. But Joshua fell upon them suddenly, having marched all night from Gilgal, and God cast great stones down upon them as they fled. Then he made the sun stand still in the sky while Joshua pursued the enemy and slaughtered every one of them, and killed all five of their kings.

So they fought on year after year, until Joshua himself was a very old man. Before he died, he divided the territories that had been captured between the twelve tribes of Israel. Certain cities and pasturelands were given separately to the Levites, who were their priests; and other cities were named as places of refuge; but the tabernacle of the Ark remained the central place of worship for the Israelites, wherever it might be. Then Joshua gathered his people together beside a great oak tree at Shechem, which was a holy place of the Canaanites. "You are witnesses," he said to them, "that you have chosen to serve the Lord our God, and not the god of this place, who is called Baal!"

"We are witnesses," replied the Israelites.

"Then, remember," he said, "that God brought you through the wilderness and gave you this land! Obey him always!"

And the people said, "We will always serve the Lord our God."

# Deborah the Judge

**D**espite the warnings of Moses and of Joshua, the people of Israel were not faithful to the Lord. They followed the customs of the Canaanites, they married Canaanite women, and in time they began to worship the Canaanite gods. After their time in the desert, this new land seemed wonderfully pleasant and comfortable, so it was easy for them to forget God and to ignore his stern commandments. Again and again the anger of the Lord was aroused against the Israelites. In many of their battles they were defeated, when he withheld his favor; and finally some of them were sold as slaves to Jabin, a Canaanite monarch whose army was led by a fierce warrior named Sisera.

Military leaders called judges had arisen among the people of Israel by now, and the judge at this time was a woman by the name of Deborah. Under a palm tree she sat in the hill country of Ephraim, and the people came to her for advice. One day, Deborah sent for Barak, an Israelite soldier, and said to him, "The Lord commands you to go with your troops and meet Sisera at the river; and he will help you defeat Sisera there." Barak replied, "If you will go with me, then I will go. Otherwise, I will not!" And Deborah said, "Very well, I will go. Even so, you will win no glory, for the Lord will deliver Sisera into the hands of a woman!"

So Deborah went with him down from the mountain, and the

Lord came down with Barak upon the armies of Sisera at the river Kishon so that they were utterly defeated. All their nine hundred chariots of iron were destroyed, and Sisera himself fled alone, on foot.

Sisera came to the tent of a woman named Jael, and she pretended to welcome him. "Stop here with me," she said, "do not be afraid." When he asked for water to drink, she gave him

milk; and she hid him in her tent, covering him with a rug. Sisera soon fell sound asleep. Then Jael took a hammer in her hand, and she crept close to him. With the hammer and a tent peg she crushed his skull, and the mighty Sisera died. Then Deborah sang a song of victory:

> Hear, O kings, O princes,
> How I bless the Lord!
> I sing to the Lord, the God of Israel!
> He has come from afar to help his people,
> And they have marched with the Lord against the mighty!
>
> Tell of the time of Israel's distress,
> The time of new gods and war within the gates,
> Before Deborah arose, as a mother to the people!
> Tell of it, you who ride on tawny asses,
> You who sit on rich carpets, who walk by the way,
> Sing of it to the sound of music, at the oases!
>
> Tell how Israel fought the Kings of Canaan,
> How the rushing waters of Kishon swept them away.
> Most blessed of women is Jael, who conquered Sisera!
> He fell at her feet, he fell down, and he died.
>
> Even now his mother gazes from her window,
> Wondering why his chariot does not come.
> Surely he has won his battle, she imagines!
> Even now, he must be dividing the spoils!
> Even now, he is seizing the Israelite maidens!
> O Lord, may all your enemies perish so!

# Gideon and the Midianites

**I**n the days of the judges, the people of Israel continued to displease the Lord God; and he gave them over for seven years into the power of the Midianites. Thick as locusts, these nomads came across the river Jordan from the east and laid waste to the new farms and the young crops of the Israelites. Finally the people retreated to mountain caves and cried to the Lord in distress.

"It was I who brought you out of Egypt," God replied, "and it was I who gave this land to you. Yet you have forgotten me and my laws; I have seen you bowing down to the gods of the Canaanites." Still, he was moved with pity for them, and one day he appeared, in the form of an angelic messenger, to a young Israelite named Gideon.

"The Lord is with you, valiant warrior," he said. "Pardon me, sir," replied Gideon, "but if God is with us, why are we in such sore distress? I think he has abandoned us to the Midianites!" The Lord answered, "Go now, Gideon, and save your nation from these people!" But Gideon replied, "How can I do such a thing? My clan is the weakest in this tribe, and I am the least important member of my family!"

"You shall do it because I am with you," said the Lord. Gideon thought for a moment, and he began to tremble. *Who is this man?* he wondered. Then he asked his visitor to stay for a moment while he prepared a meal to offer him. "Please," he asked, "wait here and give me some sign when I come back." Gideon returned with meat, broth and unleavened bread, and he placed them on a rock. The angel reached out his staff. At its touch, the rock burst into flame and Gideon's offering was consumed. The young man fell to his knees. "Peace be with you," said the angel.

That night, the Lord came again to Gideon and told him that he must tear down the altar to Baal and the sacred post beside it that his own father had built. There he must build an altar to the God of Israel, and make a sacrifice. Gideon was frightened, but he obeyed. He did his work secretly by night; and when the townspeople found it in the morning they were outraged. *Gideon must die,* they said. But his father stood firm at Gideon's side. "Let anyone who is for Baal be put to death instead!" he cried. "If Baal is a god, let him plead for himself!" And after this, Gideon became a leader and a judge.

Meanwhile, the Midianites had been joined by other armies from the east, and they lay camped nearby on the plains. Gideon said to the Lord, "I pray you, give me another sign that you truly mean for me to deliver Israel. See now, I spread out this fleece on the threshing floor. If the dew falls only onto the fleece, and the rest of the floor is dry, then I shall know what you intend for me." And in the morning, the floor of the threshing place was dry, but Gideon wrung a cupful of dew from the fleece. His heart soared, and he sounded his horn to his warriors. From all sides they came to help him do battle.

Once again now, God spoke to Gideon. "You have brought too many fighting men," he said. "I want it known that it was I, not your warriors, who won for Israel. Tell them that any man who is frightened must go home." So Gideon put them to this test, and a number of men left. "There are still too many," the Lord said. "You must put them to another test that I will show you." So Gideon did. All the remaining men were brought to the riverbank, and those who took water up in their hands to drink were allowed to stay, but those who knelt to drink from the stream were sent home. With only three hundred men now, Gideon set out to defeat the Midianite hordes.

They attacked at night, carrying flaming torches, and some loudly sounded their trumpets while others shouted the battle cry "For God and for Gideon!" The terrified armies of the Midianites awoke and fled, turning their swords against one another in their confusion. It was a tremendous rout; the forces of Gideon chased them all the way across the Jordan. And Gideon captured their kings and slaughtered them, taking the golden earrings from their bodies and the golden crescents from their camels' necks.

Then the warriors of Israel said to Gideon, "Rule over us and be our king!" But Gideon replied, "I shall not be your king, nor shall my son. Your only king shall be the Lord God!" Then he spread out his cloak and asked each man to put a golden ring there from his spoils; and from all this gold, Gideon made a statue for the village where he lived. At first the people admired the statue; then they worshiped it. After his death, Gideon's own family bowed down to it. And so, once more, the Lord God and his commandments were forgotten by the people of Israel. They remembered the good deeds of Gideon without thankfulness; and in time, they took Baal for their god again.

# Jephthah's Daughter

There once was a judge of Israel whose name was Jephthah; and of all that he loved in the world, he cared most for the dear young daughter who was his only child. It happened one day that Jephthah found himself behind enemy lines, fighting the King of the Ammonites; and he made a vow to God, saying, "O Lord, if I may win this battle I will give the first person I meet when I come home, to be offered up to you as a holy sacrifice!"

Jephthah defeated the Ammonites and returned in triumph to his village. But as he came to his house, there was his beloved daughter dancing to the sound of timbrels, hastening out to meet him in her joy at his victory. When Jephthah saw her, he tore his garments in anguish and cried, "O my daughter—must it be you? I have spoken a sacred vow that cannot be unsaid!"

When she heard what had happened, the young girl said, "Keep your vow, Father. Only grant me one wish before I am sacrificed. Let me go away for a time with my companions, so that I may mourn because I must die a maiden, never having known a man or borne a child!" Sorrowfully, he let her go; and so she spent the last days of her life, grieving in the mountains of Gilead. And for many years after this, all the maidens of Israel left their homes for four days every year to lament the fate of Jephthah's daughter.

# Samson

In the days when there were no kings in Israel, every man did as he pleased. The people's heroes were sometimes very foolish, and they were often very violent men. This is the story of a man of great power called Samson, whose strength was given by God and then taken away.

It was during the time of the Philistines, when for forty years they ruled Israel. The angel of the Lord came to a woman of the Danite tribe and said to her, "You grieve because you have no child; but soon you shall bear a son set apart from all others by God so that he may help free this nation! He must live a pure life for this, and he must never cut his hair."

So Samson was born, but he became a wild young man. Roaming about the countryside one day, he was attacked by a lion. Though he had no weapon, he picked up the beast and tore it apart with his bare hands. Then, in a nearby town, he saw a Philistine woman and fell in love with her. "Can you find no wife among our own people?" his parents asked. "Must you go to these unholy Philistines, who plunder us?" But Samson replied, "She pleases me, and I will have her."

A wedding was planned, and on the way to the celebration Samson stopped to look at the carcass of the lion he had killed. He saw that some bees had built a hive in the carcass and made honey there; so he took the honey up in his hands and ate it as he walked. When he arrived at the wedding feast, Samson said to the guests, "Here is a riddle! If you cannot tell me the answer, you must pay a price:

> *Out of the eater came something to eat*
> *Out of the strong came something sweet*
> *What were they?"*

Three days went by, and still the people could not guess. On the fourth day they went to his bride and begged her to find out the answer. So the crafty Philistine woman pretended to weep in his arms and whispered to Samson, "You do not love me if you will not tell me the answer!" And she teased him this way until, on the seventh day, he finally told her; and she told the wedding guests; and they told Samson, "It was the lion and it was the honey!" Samson was furious. He called off the wedding and went raging out into a field, where he caught three hundred foxes and tied torches to their tails. He drove the foxes into the Philistines' crops, and destroyed them all.

The Philistines came after Samson, and again he had no weapon, but he took up the jawbone of an ass, and with that he slew a thousand men. After this, Samson went on to Gaza, where he saw another Philistine woman who pleased him. So he went into her house while the men of the town waited outside to capture him. But Samson rose up at midnight; and he seized the gate of the town and tore it off, posts and all, and carried it away.

Finally Samson fell in love with a third Philistine woman. This one was the most cunning and treacherous of all; and her name was Delilah. "Find out for us," the Philistines begged Delilah, "what is the secret of this man's power! How can we bind him and tame him?"

106

"I will find out," said Delilah. And every night, she begged and teased Samson to tell her, and every night, he gave her a false answer. "Bind me with seven bowstrings," he told her; and another time he said, "Bind me with new ropes; then I will lose my strength and be like any other man." Delilah tried everything he suggested, but he always escaped. Finally Samson confessed to her, "My hair has never been cut because of a vow to the Lord from my birth, and that is the source of my strength!" So Delilah took his head in her lap, and when he had fallen asleep she cut off his hair. And then the power of Samson left him.

She called in the Philistines and they seized him. They gouged out his eyes, and then they bound him with chains of bronze and put him to work in the mill at Gaza, turning the great wheel. Day after day, night after night Samson labored, blind and in pain; yet during this time, his hair began to grow back again.

"Send Samson out to amuse us," the Philistines cried one day. "We want to make sport of him!" So he was brought out, but he said to the boy who led him, "Bring me to the pillars of this building so that I may lean upon them," and the boy did. Then Samson cried out to God, "Lord, give me strength once more!" and he put his arms around the pillars and pulled with all his might.

The building came tumbling down upon Samson, and upon all the chiefs of the Philistines who were standing there, and upon all the great crowd of people who were there to mock him. Every one of them was killed on the spot, and Samson died too; but in his death he defeated the enemies of Israel at last, and in his death was his victory.

# *Ruth*

From Bethlehem, in Judah, a man named Elimelech went up into the land of Moab to escape a famine that threatened Israel; and this was in the ancient days of the judges. He brought with him his wife, Naomi, and their two sons; and in time the sons grew up and married Moabite women. But Elimelech died, and the two young men died, so that Naomi was left alone in a strange country with her two daughters-in-law, who were foreigners.

"I must go back to the land of my people, in Judah," she told her daughters-in-law, "and you shall return now, each to your mother's house. I have been struck down by the Lord; I have nothing more to offer you but the hope that he will be as kind to you as you have been to me and the men who have died."

Now, one of Naomi's daughters-in-law was named Orpah, which means "she who turns away," and the other was named Ruth, which means "the bountiful one." When Orpah heard her mother-in-law's command, she wept, and kissed Naomi, and went, as she had been told to do, back to the home of her childhood. But Ruth clung to Naomi and would not leave her. "Look," said Naomi, "your sister-in-law has gone back to her own people and her own god. Follow her now, for you must do the same!"

But Ruth said to Naomi, "Do not ask me again, I pray you, to leave your side or turn from your company. For wherever you go, there will I go also; and wherever you dwell, that shall be my home. Your people shall be my people; and your God shall be my God. Wherever you die, there will I die and be buried. May I suffer the wrath of the Lord if I part from you, even in death!"

Naomi saw that she could not be persuaded, and so the two women traveled toward Judah together. They arrived at the time of the harvest, when Hebrew law allowed the poor to follow the reapers in the fields and take for themselves whatever was left. "Let me glean after the reapers and try to find the owner of some field who might show me kindness," Ruth said to Naomi. "Go, my daughter," Naomi said to her.

Now, in Bethlehem at this time there lived a man called Boaz, a close kinsman of Elimelech's. He was a kind and gentle man a good deal older than Ruth, and he was very rich. When he saw her hard at work in the hot sun, gleaning his fields, he asked his servants about Ruth, and he was deeply moved by the story they told him. He went to Ruth and told her, "Stay close to my maidens, my dear, and when you are thirsty, ask my young men for some water to drink. They will not trouble you." Ruth bowed low to him and thanked him from her heart.

When it was time for the midday meal, Boaz said to her, "Come here, my daughter, and eat some of this bread. Dip it into the wine if you wish." Ruth ate her fill and kept some to bring to Naomi; then she asked Boaz, "My lord, how have I found favor in your sight, since I am a foreigner?" And Boaz replied, "I know all that you have done for your mother-in-law, and I know of your courage in coming to a strange country. You have taken refuge in the God of Israel now; and he shall reward you, and he shall shelter you under his wings."

Rejoicing, Ruth went to Naomi and told her all that had happened. "Blessed be Boaz!" Naomi cried. "He is my dead husband's kinsman, and he will help us to reclaim our land." Then she told Ruth how to approach Boaz, according to the customs of the Israelites. All through the harvest, Ruth saw Boaz watching over her; and when it was done, she went to him at night where he was sleeping. She lay at his feet, and when he waked, she asked him to cover her with his cloak. "May you be blessed by the Lord," said he, "for you have not chosen any of the men outside the clan, whether poor or rich! I will have you as my wife if I can persuade our kinsmen, for everyone knows that you are a woman of great worth. Stay now, and no one shall know of it."

So she lay at his feet until it was nearly dawn, and then Boaz arose to speak with the elders of the town. "According to our customs, Ruth has asked for my protection. I am not the nearest kinsman, yet I wish to marry her," he said.

After much negotiation this was arranged, and so the inheritance of Ruth was saved, and the land of Naomi was restored also. It was a day of great joy when Ruth and Boaz were married. Soon they had a son, and the women of Bethlehem said to Naomi, "Thanks be to God, you are no longer left without kin! Your daughter-in-law who loves you has been more to you than seven sons. And now this baby will be the comfort of your old age!" So they gave the boy to Naomi to nurse, and they named him Obed. And Obed became the father of Jesse; and Jesse was the father of David, the great and mighty king of Israel.

# Samuel

There was a woman named Hannah, whose husband dearly loved her, but she was unhappy and ashamed because she could not have a child. Now, at this time the Ark of the Covenant was kept at Shiloh, and Hannah went there to pray. "O Lord, look upon the misery of your handmaiden!" she begged. "Send me a son and I will give him into your service forever!" The Lord God heard her prayer and took pity on her; soon Hannah gave birth to a fine baby boy. She named him Samuel, and this was her song of joy:

> My heart exults in the Lord,
> For he is my salvation.
> He humbles the proud and the mighty,
> He comforts the barren and raises up the poor!
>
> It is not through our own strength that we overcome,
> It is through the Lord God, who made the world;
> And he will guard the footsteps of the faithful,
> And he will give power to his King, to his anointed!

When Samuel was still very young, his parents took him to the temple of God at Shiloh to be trained as a priest, in fulfillment of Hannah's vow. His mother gave him a little tunic of linen to wear; and every year when she came to visit him, she brought him a larger one that she had made.

Meantime, Samuel helped Eli, the chief priest at Shiloh, with his duties. Eli, who was a good-hearted man, was worried because his own sons, who also served at the shrine, were wicked young men. The wrath of the Lord, he knew, might soon come to destroy his entire household. But he was old and weak; he scolded his sons from time to time, but he did not make them behave.

God almost never revealed himself in those days, or spoke to anyone. Young Samuel was lying in the sanctuary of the Ark one night while the lamp was still burning and Eli was in his own room, nearby. Suddenly the boy heard a voice calling, "Samuel! Samuel!" and he ran to Eli, answering, "Here I am!" But Eli said, "I did not call you. Go back and lie down." Then, a second time, Samuel heard his name called, and again Eli said, "I did not speak." When the boy heard the voice calling him a third time, the old priest knew who it must be. He said to Samuel, "If someone calls again, you must answer, 'Speak, Lord, for your servant is listening.' "

Once more the voice called, "Samuel! Samuel!" and the boy replied as he had been taught. The Lord came into the sanctuary then and stood beside Samuel. "The House of Eli is condemned," he said. "His sons have cursed me and defiled the shrine, yet he has not corrected them. Tell him this!" Then the Lord went away and Samuel lay very still all night, frightened to tell Eli what he had heard. In the morning he found courage at last to repeat the words, and the old man said sadly, "It is the Lord who has spoken! May he do what he thinks best."

After this, God continued to visit Samuel, and as he grew to manhood he became known far and wide as a great prophet. But the end of the House of Eli was at hand. When the Philistines attacked again, they defeated the Israelites and seized the Ark from them. A messenger ran into Shiloh with the news, and met Eli, who was very feeble and quite blind by now. "The army is in flight," the messenger cried, "and both your sons are killed!" When Eli heard this, and when he learned that the Ark, which was the glory of Israel, had been taken, he fell down from the place where he was sitting beside a gate, and his neck was broken, and he died.

All Israel mourned the capture of the Ark. However, it brought great trouble to the enemy. First it was placed in the Philistines' temple, and the statue of their own god, Dagon, fell immediately into ruins. Then it was moved about, and all the Philistines who went near it were struck by plague. At last they decided to return the Ark, with golden offerings of remorse to the God of Israel; and by this time, it was Samuel who ruled as judge.

Traveling among his people now, helping them with their problems and their disputes, Samuel found that many had turned to the worship of Baal and Astarte and other foreign idols; yet he saw that they yearned in their hearts for the Lord God. Again the Philistines struck. Samuel cried to the people, "Set your hearts on God alone! The Lord God of Hosts will surely deliver you!"

The people were sorry for their unfaithfulness. They begged for mercy and they begged the Lord to help them, while Samuel sent up sacrifices and prayers on their behalf. At this the Philistines fled, and for a time there was peace in the land.

After a number of years the Israelites came to Samuel and said, "You are growing old, and your sons do not follow our ways. Choose a king for us, for we want to have a leader like other nations." Samuel was troubled, and he asked the Lord's advice. "Obey the people," said the Lord. "Give them a king; I will show you the man."

# Given a King

One day soon after, a handsome young Benjaminite named Saul was sent by his father into the countryside to find some mules that had strayed. Through Ephraim he wandered and into the land of Zuph, searching without success. Finally Saul came to Ramah, where Samuel lived, and hearing of his wisdom, came to consult him. "I have been expecting you," Samuel said to the astonished young man. "As for the mules you lost three days ago, do not worry about them. They are found and they will be returned. Furthermore, all Israel shall be put into your hands!"

Speechless with wonder, Saul found himself treated at Samuel's own table that night to the Lord's portion that had been set aside; and in the morning the prophet walked with his guest to the edge of the town. There he anointed Saul's head with holy oil. "Go home now," he said to Saul, "and await the signs that God will send. For you are the prince who must rule over our people; you are the warrior who must save us from our enemies."

# Saul: A Troubled Monarch

**M**any signs appeared, showing the people that the spirit of the Lord was in Saul. They made him their king, and during his first battle, which was with the Ammonites, he showed them that he was a fierce warrior. After the victory, Samuel said, "Here indeed is your king! And yet, beware. Never forget that it was God who led you out of Egypt. Remember that it was God who sent Moses to you, and the judges. Only he is the Lord! He will strike you down if your king does not obey him."

At first Saul was a fine leader, careful at all times to obey the laws of God. He defeated the Moabites and the Edomites and the people of many other nations. The Israelites had very few weapons made of iron at this time, but the Philistines had powerful iron swords and shields, so that they were the most terrible of enemies. As Jonathan, the son of Saul, grew up, he came to fight beside his father in the field. Against the Philistines he scored a brilliant triumph; and yet when the boy dared to break a sacred fast, Saul did not hesitate to punish him.

One day Samuel told Saul, "The Lord God has spoken! He orders you to attack the Amalekites. They slaughtered our people when we were coming out of Egypt. Now they shall be punished and utterly destroyed!"

And so Saul gathered his warriors by the thousands, and they lay at ambush beside the city of Amalek. He sent a message telling some Kenite people who were within the city to flee, for they had shown kindness in the past to the Israelites. When the Kenites had left, Saul attacked Amalek and, in obedience to God's command, reduced it to ruins; and the king and all the people were killed. But Saul saw that his soldiers wanted to bring some of the finest of the sheep and cattle with them, and he let them take these animals home, after the battle.

"What is this bleating of lambs and bellowing of oxen I hear in my ears?" cried Samuel. "You have not obeyed the Lord!" Saul replied, "But I did obey! I destroyed the city. I let the men save only these creatures, so that they might sacrifice them to God, here with me." But Samuel was furious. "Is the pleasure of the Lord in burnt offerings and sacrifices—or is it in obedience to his word?" he cried. "You are the anointed king of Israel! You knew that everything in that city was God's to burn by your hand then and there, but you wanted it your own way. You wanted to please the people! You rejected God, and he rejects you now. You are no longer wanted as our king." And he turned away from Saul.

Saul reached out to grasp the edge of Samuel's robe. "I have sinned," he whispered. "But please, show me some respect! Do not shame me now, in front of everyone." So Samuel went to the altar with Saul and worshiped, but he grieved at the failure of the man he had anointed; and from that time on, Saul was a deeply troubled man. The spirit of the Lord had left him, and his heart was tormented by a sense of gloom and terror, day and night.

# The Shepherd Boy

One day, the Lord said to Samuel, "It is time for you to stop mourning for Saul. I have already chosen a new king for Israel among the sons of Jesse, and I will show him to you so that you may anoint him. Fill your horn with oil, Samuel, and go!"

So the prophet took up his staff and walked to Bethlehem, carrying the holy oil, and he came to the house of Jesse, who was the grandson of Boaz and Ruth. By now, Jesse was an old man with seven fine sons at his side; and the firstborn was unusually tall and good-looking. When Samuel saw him, he thought, "Surely this is God's choice!" But the Lord said to him, "Pay no attention— I have rejected that one. God does not see as man sees. Men look at the appearance, but the Lord looks at the heart."

One by one, all seven of Jesse's sons were presented to Samuel, but he was certain that God had chosen none of them. Puzzled, he asked his host, "Have you any more sons?" And Jesse replied, "Oh, yes, there is one more, but he is just a young boy, out watching the sheep." "Send for him," said Samuel. Soon David came in, a fresh-faced youth with beautiful, sparkling eyes.

Samuel looked at David standing quietly there among his brothers, and he listened deep in his heart for the word of the Lord. Then he said, "Come, I will anoint him; for this is the one."

# David and Goliath

**K**ing Saul paced the hall of his palace, sick with grief and fear, until his servants came to him at last and said, "Let us find someone to play soothing music for you, so that you may soon be healed of this terrible sadness"; and the king consented.

Now, during his long days and nights alone in the fields tending his father's flocks, young David had become a poet and musician of great skill. So it was he who came at the bidding of Saul's servants; and when he played his lyre for Saul, peace entered the heart of the tormented man. He came to love David very dearly, and demanded often to have him at his side.

At this time the Philistines pressed upon Israel's armies with fearsome power, and there came from their ranks a mighty warrior named Goliath, a giant of a man who challenged any one of them to single combat. The loser, he said, should surrender his own people as slaves. The Israelites trembled at the very sight of Goliath, for he was ten feet tall. He wore a helmet of bronze and a heavy coat of mail; and he carried a spear as large as a weaver's beam, with an iron point upon it weighing more than seventeen pounds.

It happened that David was sent into the Israelite camp to bring food for his older brothers, who were in the front lines, and

he heard the shouts and curses of the Philistine giant. "Who is this?" he asked in astonishment. "Who dares to insult the army of the Lord God of Hosts?" David's eldest brother, Eliab, sneered at him, "Go home, shepherd boy, and mind your sheep!" "What have I done?" asked David. "Am I not even allowed to speak?"

And he went back to King Saul and told him, "I will go against Goliath myself, and I will win. When bears and lions try to attack my father's sheep, I can always kill them. This Philistine is no more than a great beast, and God will surely deliver him into my hands."

"You are only a boy!" cried Saul. "This man has been a warrior from his youth!" When he saw that David was determined, he put his own armor on the lad and gave him his own sword; but David had trouble moving about. "I am not used to these things," he told the king, and took them off. Then he went into battle wearing his tunic with his staff in his hand; and he carried his sling, and into his shepherd's pouch he put five smooth stones that he had chosen carefully from the riverbed.

Goliath roared with laughter when he saw David approaching. "Come, little one," he called, "I will give your flesh to the birds of the air and the beasts of the field!" But as he was still shouting at David, the boy ran quickly forward and hurled one of the stones with his sling. The stone smashed deep into Goliath's forehead; his blood gushed forth, and he fell face down in all his armor, on the ground. Then David ran up and seized the giant's own sword, and cut off his head with it. A tremendous cheer went up from the Israelites, and the Philistine army turned and fled.

# The Outlaw

When King Saul learned that David had killed Goliath, he was so overjoyed that he immediately gave the boy a position of high command in his armies, and they went on to further victories. The warriors loved David, and the king's son Jonathan came to love the young hero as if their two souls were one.

It happened that Saul was witness one day to a great

celebration among the people. The women danced and sang with their timbrels and their lyres:

> *Saul has killed his thousands*
> *And David his tens of thousands!*

At this, a new shadow fell upon the heart of the troubled king. Saul's greatest weakness was that he cared too much what people thought of him, and not enough for God. Now that the spirit of the Lord had left him, he was desperately anxious to be first in the eyes of all his followers; and so from this time on he looked upon David with jealousy and fear.

And now young Michal, the daughter of King Saul, fell in love with David. Furiously, the king thought to himself, "Well, there will be a way to use this against him! To win her hand in marriage, I

shall send David into battle; it will be one that he cannot win, and the Philistines will kill him for me." But David won this battle too, and then came back to claim his promised bride.

The spirit of terror took full command now over King Saul. Day and night, he sighed and trembled and could not sleep. When David came, as was usual at such times, to play gentle melodies for him, Saul flew into a rage. He hurled his spear at David where he sat with his lyre; but David dodged, and the spear went into the wall; so he escaped with his life.

That night, David's wife, Michal, said to him, "You must flee from here or you will be killed tomorrow!" and she helped him to climb down from their window while it was dark. When the king's soldiers came to arrest him, she pointed to a bundle she had arranged in their bed and said, "David is sick!" So the men went away and did not find out until later that he had run in the night to Ramah, to hide with the prophet Samuel.

After this, David came back in secret to talk with Jonathan. "What have I done?" he asked his friend. "Why does your father want to kill me?" Jonathan replied, "I cannot believe it. He has told me nothing. But on my solemn vow of brotherhood with you, I will help you in any way I can!"

It was the feast of the new moon the following day, and the two set up a signal between them that would tell David whether or not his life was still in danger. Jonathan went, as planned, to the king's table while David hid in a nearby field beside a certain heap of stones. When David's name was mentioned at the celebration, Saul turned upon Jonathan and shouted, "You son of an evil mother! I know that you care for David and you plot with him! You are in disgrace, and the son of Jesse is condemned to death!" Hot with anger, Jonathan rose from the table without touching his food, and went out into the fields. He took up his bow and sent an arrow into the air so that it fell beyond the heap of stones. This was the signal that David must flee to save himself.

But David waited until they were unobserved and then he came out from his hiding place, weeping, and embraced his friend. "Go in peace," said Jonathan, also in tears. "God will be witness of our love for one another, now and forever!"

So it was that David went into the wilderness and became an outlaw, gathering warriors of his own to fight in the deserts and the mountain passes. Time after time, Saul sent his armies out to capture David, but he always escaped them. At Horesh, in the land of Zuph, one day, Jonathan and David met once more. "Take courage," Jonathan told him, "for you shall be the next king of Israel, and I shall be second in command to you. I believe my father knows this too."

Again the two friends parted, and David took his band of men to the stronghold of Engedi, a mountain fortress that was later known as Masada. There they hid themselves away in the back of a deep cave, and it happened that King Saul himself came for shelter at the front of the same cave. David was so close to the king that he could have killed him easily. Instead, he quietly cut off the border of Saul's cloak. Then, when Saul had left the cave, David stood up on the rock and shouted after him, "My lord King, look what I have taken from you, and yet I spared your life! How can you believe that I mean you any harm?"

King Saul looked up at him and called, "Is that you, my son David? Then, you are a better man than I. May God reward you! Now I know that you will rule Israel, and rule it well." And he wept.

# The Witch of Endor

When the prophet Samuel died, the whole of Israel gathered to mourn him, and he was buried where he had lived, in the town of Ramah. Soon afterward, the Philistines came with a tremendous army to attack King Saul, and he was terrified. After a day and a night of being unable to touch his food, he told his men, "Find me a witch who can summon up spirits. I will go to her in secret and learn what I must do."

Now, Saul himself had outlawed witchcraft in Israel; nevertheless his men found a woman in Endor who practiced the magic arts. Saul went to her by night in disguise, but she saw immediately that he was the king, and she was frightened. "I swear by the Lord," promised Saul, "that you shall come to no harm; only summon up the spirit of Samuel for me. I must ask his advice!" So the woman obeyed, and in a moment she whispered to Saul, "I see an old man rising up in a cloak!"

It was the ghost of Samuel. "Why have you disturbed my rest?" cried the ghost. "God has abandoned you, Saul! Tomorrow you shall be with me here in the land of the spirits. And tomorrow your sons shall be with me too, for the Philistines shall slaughter you!" When he heard this, King Saul fell to the ground in a swoon of terror at the feet of the Witch of Endor.

At Mount Gilboa, in heavy fighting, King Saul and three of his sons were surrounded. The soldiers of Israel were being slaughtered on all sides. Jonathan and his brothers were killed; and at last, in despair, the king fell upon his own sword and killed himself.

When the news was brought to David, he cried out and tore his clothes in anguish. Then he rose up with his lyre and composed a psalm of grief and praise for the dead. *Alas, the glory of Israel has been slain,* he sang,

> *Tell it not in Gath,*
> *Publish it not in the streets of Askelon,*
> *Lest the Philistines rejoice.*
> *Lo, how the mighty are fallen!*
> *Saul and Jonathan, swifter than eagles,*
> *Stronger than lions!*
> *O Jonathan, I am desolate for you—*
> *Lo, how the mighty are fallen.*

After the worst of his grief had passed, David asked the Lord, "Where shall I go now?" and God told him to go up to Hebron, in the land of Judah. There, at the age of thirty, David was anointed king; but other tribes wanted to crown one of Saul's surviving sons, and so there was a long war after this between the House of David and the House of Saul. Seven years later, all the tribes came together and said to David, "The Lord has told you that you shall be our ruler. You are our flesh and blood, and you led us into battle in the old days. So be it!"

At last the kingdom of Israel was united, and David began his long and glorious reign. His first great conquest for his people was the capture of Jerusalem. The city was already very ancient in those days. It was centrally placed, between the northern and the southern Israelite tribes, and it had been the last stronghold of the Canaanites, so its surrender was the cause of tremendous joy among the people of Israel.

"The Ark of the Covenant belongs here now," King David said, and he gathered up the finest of his troops to help him bring the Ark into the city. The people took up their lyres, their harps, their tambourines and their castanets and their cymbals; and they made a great procession with the Ark as it rolled along, in a fine new cart pulled by oxen, on the road to Jerusalem. When they entered the city, they sounded their rams' horns, and sang and danced with all their might. King David himself danced before the Lord that day in the streets of Jerusalem, dressed in a priest's linen loincloth and whirling in ecstasy. The Ark was placed in a tent that he had pitched for it, and he made solemn sacrifices, prayers and ceremonies. Before the people departed he gave them each some bread and figs and a raisin cake.

Now, David's wife, Michal, was watching all this from her window, and when she saw David dancing and whirling, she despised him in her heart. "You are the king of Israel!" she shouted at him when he came home. "How could you expose yourself before the common people and make such a fool of yourself?" David answered her, "I was not dancing for the people, I was dancing for God. He chose me! I shall be a fool for God many times, my dear. You may not like it, but the people you call common, will."

And it was true that the people greatly loved David, not only for his power as a warrior and a poet, but for his fairness, his noble spirit and his loving heart. David was generous to the family of Saul, although Saul had been a dangerous enemy. Finding that Jonathan had left a crippled son, he called for the young man to sit

at the royal table with him, and he gave him land and property.

The prophet Nathan, who was a wise and holy man, was a close friend to whom David often turned for advice. One day soon after the Ark had come to Jerusalem, David said to Nathan, "I live in a house of cedar, while God's word dwells in a tent. Shall I build a better house for the Ark?" Nathan replied, "Do what is in your heart, for the Lord is with you." But, that night, God came to Nathan and said, "Tell David that I have not lived in a house since I brought my people out of Egypt, and I have never asked for one. Tell him that I took him from the fields where he was a shepherd and made him the king of Israel, so I will build him a house instead. But this house shall not be a building. It shall be a family to live after him, the *House of David.* And if his descendants obey my laws, I shall keep them always safe from their enemies, and his

kingdom shall endure forever!" When David heard this, he uttered a great prayer of praise and thanksgiving to God.

In the field, against the enemies of Israel, King David continued to be successful, for wherever he fought, the Lord God was with him. One day in the springtime, however, David had stayed at home while his troops were at the borders. Toward evening he rose from his couch and went to walk upon the palace roof, and from there he saw a beautiful woman bathing. "Who is that?" he asked his servants. "That is Bathsheba," they said, "wife of your soldier Uriah the Hittite." King David was filled with desire for the woman; he sent for her, and she came to his bed while her husband was at war. Soon Bathsheba told the king that she was going to bear his child, and he began to plot a way to get rid of Uriah. "Send the Hittite into the front lines," he told his commander, "and then move away from him while he is hard-pressed." They did, and Uriah fell at the hands of the enemy.

Now David took Bathsheba as his queen, and their son was born. But the prophet Nathan had seen all that had happened, and he risked his life against the king's anger to tell him boldly that he had sinned. "You have broken the Lord's commandments," he told David. "And he shall destroy the child because of it!"

David was stricken with remorse and shame. When his son became ill soon afterward, King David lay on the bare ground in sackcloth, fasting and praying continually that God might spare the child. His officers could do nothing with him, and when the boy died, after seven days, they were afraid to tell the king. To their surprise, David rose up when he heard the news, saying, "It is finished, and I cannot bring him back. I have grieved and I have prayed for him; now I can do no more." He washed and anointed himself; then he put on fresh clothes and went to his wife, Bathsheba, to comfort her. And in time Bathsheba bore him another son, who lived. This was Solomon, future ruler of the House of David, and of Israel.

# David and Absalom

As it was the custom among kings during those days, David had many wives and many children; and the quarrels between them were sometimes very bitter. Of all King David's sons the most troublesome was Absalom. As a youth he was banished from court for taking the law into his own hands; and when his father had mercy on him and welcomed him back, Absalom still did not change his ways. With craft and charm he convinced the people that he should be a judge and a military leader; and when many flocked to his cause, he decided that it was he, not his father, who should rule Israel.

A messenger came now to David and said, "The hearts of the people have turned to Absalom, and we are in great danger. He has an army with him now!" Deeply disturbed, the king left the city of Zion with his own followers and went into the wilderness between Jerusalem and the river Jordan. Many of the faithful joined him there, but others scorned him; and one day, as King David made his way through the mountains, a man named Shimei cursed him and threw stones at him. The king's soldiers were outraged. But he said to them sadly, "Let him be! After all, my own son wants to see me killed!" And he cried out to God in his great distress,

*Lord how many are turning against me!*
*O God, my glory, my encircling shield —*
*Arise and save me from my enemies!*

Across the river Jordan the armies of Absalom pursued him, and King David saw that he must take a stand. Near the forest of Ephraim he told his men, "We must fight them now, but when you come upon Absalom in battle, be gentle with him for my sake!"

The attack came. In and out of the trees and vines, the rocks and gullies of the forest, the men fought desperately, hand to hand. Soon David's army was uppermost, and Absalom was surrounded by the soldiers of the king. The mule he was riding dashed beneath the limbs of a great oak tree, and Absalom was trapped among its branches, hanging by his head and helpless to escape. The soldiers stood by, wondering what to do. Then one of David's commanders arrived on the scene. "We must not harm the king's son," the men reminded him. But Joab replied, "Out of my way! Don't waste my time with this!" and he took up his lance and slaughtered Absalom where he hung.

The battle was over, and the runners were hastening back to the town where the king waited for news. He saw them coming and cried out to them, "Is all well with young Absalom?" The first runner replied, "Good news for you! We have won the battle!" But the king cried out again, "Is all well with young Absalom?" And the second messenger, knowing that he could not hide the truth, said, "My lord King, may all your enemies meet his fate!"

David went to his chamber above the town gate and wept, "O my son Absalom! My son! I wish that I had died instead of you. Absalom, my son, my son!" And his soldiers came back victorious, but their faces burned with shame, because the king would not speak to them; he would only say over and over again, "O my son Absalom, O Absalom, my son, my son!"

# Solomon's Glory

Absalom was dead, but Solomon, the child of David's marriage to Bathsheba, was growing up now, well guarded against all rivals by his mother, who was still very beautiful and very powerful in her old age. One day, Bathsheba approached King David and, in her most charming manner, begged him to name Solomon as heir to the throne. King David granted her request, and so young Solomon was anointed in the presence of all the people. "It would not be right for me to build our holy Temple," David told the nation, "for I have been a man of battle. But my son Solomon will do it in his own time."

As a very old man David was much beloved, and at peace. The survival of Solomon was a sign to him that the worst of his sins had been forgiven; and ruling together with his son, he began preparing for the construction of the Temple. From the people and from his own treasury he collected precious materials: fine woods and rare gems, onyx and alabaster, silver and bronze and gold. His House was strong in its covenant with the Lord; he knew that it would live on after him. In public worship the people now used music and poetry that he himself had written for the love of God; and when the old warrior died, he left not only a son to guard his inheritance, but psalms of such splendor that they would be remembered long after him and to this very day. David slept at last with his ancestors, and Solomon came into full power.

Early in his reign Solomon went to Gibeon, which was the greatest of the high places, long considered holy by the people; and there he offered prayers and sacrifices to the Lord. The Lord came to him in a dream that night and said, "Solomon, ask of me what you want!" And the king replied, "I am not sure yet how to rule these people of yours, for they are such a great nation and so numerous. Please, O Lord, give your servant an understanding heart. Help me to know good from evil so that I may do your will!" And God was pleased. He said, "Solomon, you have not asked for a long life, or for riches, or for the death of your enemies. You have asked for wisdom, which is far, far better. I shall make you wiser than any other man, and because your spirit pleases me so much, I shall give you all that you did not ask of me, as well."

So it was that Solomon became a ruler marvelously wise and powerful, wealthy and also long-lived. With peace on all his borders, he organized the tribes of the north and of the south so that each person helped to serve the throne and all knew what their duties were. Like his father before him, Solomon wrote songs and prayers; he wrote proverbs, too, and his wise sayings became widely known. He knew all about plants and animals, reptiles, birds and fishes. Foreign monarchs came to visit him, bearing splendid gifts; and wealth poured into his treasuries, for he sent many ships out trading, and his people were set to work mining the precious metals of the earth. For himself and for his many wives and children, Solomon built a splendid palace, and he built a part of the great wall of Jerusalem. But his most important work was the building of the Temple, to shelter the Ark in the city of Zion.

This Temple was shaped like the tent that had been the home

of the Ark since Moses, but it was far larger and more magnificent, and it was solidly constructed. Its walls were made of cedar from Lebanon, and in the courtyard was a great sea of molten bronze resting upon twelve bronze oxen. In the most holy place within, there were tall cherubim of olive wood all sheeted over with gold, and the Ark of the Covenant had its resting place under their wings. With golden leaves and flowers the sanctuary was decorated, and it had a floor made of pure gold. When the Temple was finished, after seven years of hard labor, and the Ark was brought inside, the priests there saw the cloud of God's presence descending; and his glory shone around them so brightly that they had to turn aside their eyes.

Then the people held a solemn celebration in Jerusalem. On his knees before them, with his arms raised high, Solomon prayed, "O God of Israel, watch over this place, and remember always that it is your home! We have built you a house to dwell in; stay here with us always!" And then he said, "You know our inmost hearts, O Lord! We praise your holy name; forgive us our sins. Let your judgment upon us be merciful!" Then King Solomon stood, and blessed the people. "May we bless the Lord forever, and may we obey him without fail and keep his commandments. For we are his chosen people; we must show the world that our Lord is God, and that there is no other God except the God of Israel."

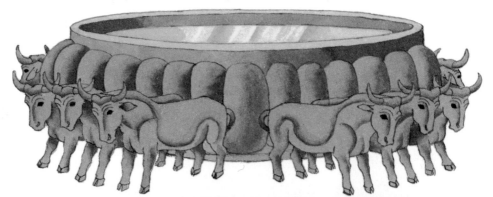

# The Wisdom of Solomon

Two women came to Solomon for help one day, and with them they brought a baby boy. "My lord King," said the first woman, "this child is mine. The other woman stole him from me while I slept, because her own baby had died. Now she says this one is hers, not mine; but I am telling the truth."

And the second woman said, "You are lying! This is my child!" And the first woman cried, "That is not true! I swear that this child, who is alive, is my own!" There in the court they stood

shouting and quarreling with all their might before the king; and everyone looked at Solomon to see what he would do.

"Bring me a sword," ordered King Solomon. And when the sword had been brought, he said, "There is a way to settle this.

Cut the living child in two; then each of you may have half of him." When she heard this, the second woman shrugged her shoulders, but the first cried out, "No! No! Let her have him if she must, but do not hurt my son!"

And King Solomon smiled. "Put away the sword," he said. "Do not hurt the child. Now we know which one is his mother. The second woman only wanted him for her own satisfaction. But it is the true mother who will bring misery upon herself before she will allow her child to suffer harm."

# The Queen of Sheba

The news of Solomon's wisdom had reached the far-away realms of Africa, and there a powerful queen decided that she would visit him and put him to the test with some difficult questions. "Can it be that these rough warriors in the north have really become civilized?" the Queen of Sheba

wondered as she prepared for her long journey. She loaded her camels with gifts for the king: gold and precious gems, spices and rare wood for the making of lyres and musical instruments. Decked in her finest jewels, her silken garments and veils and sweet perfumes, she entered Jerusalem; and she was filled with curiosity, but she did not expect to have her questions answered.

When she saw the palace of the king, and the Temple, and the magnificent ceremonies at the Temple, she was astonished; and when the Queen of Sheba saw the elegance of Solomon's court in all its glory, it took her breath away. "I would never have believed it!" she told the king. On gold plates they were served the most delicious food she had ever tasted; and they lingered together in conversation long into the night as she opened her heart to him. Solomon answered every one of her questions, and his wisdom seemed more wonderful to her than any of the gifts she had brought. "Blessed are you," she told him, "and great is the Lord God of Israel!"

# The Song of Solomon

The Song of Solomon was written in celebration of the love of man and woman, and the love of God for all Creation. Here are some of the most famous of its lines:

I am the rose of Sharon, and the lily of the valleys.

As the apple tree among the trees of the wood,

So is my beloved among the sons.

He brought me to the banqueting house,

And his banner over me was love.

I charge you, O ye daughters of Jerusalem,

By the roes, and by the hinds of the field,

That ye stir not up, nor awake my love,

Till he please.

My beloved spake, and said unto me,

Rise up, my love, my fair one, and come away.

For, lo, the winter is past, the rain is over and gone;

The flowers appear on the earth;

The time of the singing of birds is come,

And the voice of the turtle is heard in our land;

The fig tree putteth forth her green figs,

And the vines with the tender grape

Give a good smell. Arise, my love, my fair one,

And come away.

Take us the foxes, the little foxes, that spoil the vines:

For our vines have tender grapes.
My beloved is mine, and I am his:
He feedeth among the lilies.

                  \*   \*   \*

Behold, thou art fair, my love;
Behold, thou art fair;
Thou hast doves' eyes within thy locks:

*Come with me from Lebanon, my spouse:*
*Look from the top of Amana, from the top of Shenir*
*And Hermon, from the lions' dens,*
*From the mountains of the leopards.*
*Thou hast ravished my heart, my sister, my spouse;*
*Thou hast ravished my heart with one of thine eyes.*
*A garden inclosed is my sister, my spouse:*
*A fountain of gardens, a well of living waters,*
*And streams from Lebanon.*

\* \* \*

*I sleep, but my heart waketh:*
*It is the voice of my beloved; my soul failed when he spake.*
*His mouth is most sweet: yea, he is altogether lovely.*
*This is my beloved, and this is my friend,*
*O daughters of Jerusalem.*
*Come, my beloved, let us go forth into the field;*
*Let us get up early to the vineyards;*
*At our gates are all manner of pleasant fruits,*
*New and old, which I have laid up for thee.*
*Make haste, my beloved,*
*And be thou like to a roe or to a young hart*
*Upon the mountains of spices.*
*Set me as a seal upon thine heart,*
*As a seal upon thine arm;*
*Many waters cannot quench love,*
*Neither can the floods drown it.*
*Love is strong as death.*

(from the King James Version)

# A Kingdom Divided

The kingdom of Solomon was very powerful, and Solomon was wealthy indeed, and very wise; nevertheless he made some serious mistakes. In the building of the Temple, he forced a great many of his people to work as slaves, so that rebellion was brewing against the throne even during his lifetime. And he brought foreign gods and idols into Jerusalem together with the many, many women he loved and married during his reign. The daughter of the Egyptian Pharaoh was one of his brides; there were also Moabites and Edomites, and princesses of other nations. Some of these he wed mainly in order to keep their people friendly toward Israel; but as he grew older, Solomon's heart softened more and more, and his wits were won over by the opinions of his wives. He built shrines in his kingdom to Chemosh, the god of the Moabites, and to Milcom, the abominable god of the Ammonite people; he himself became a follower of Astarte, who was the goddess of the Sidonians, so that the jealous anger of the Lord was aroused.

When Solomon died, leaving his son Rehoboam as his heir, this new king from the House of David wondered how he should rule the nation. But instead of asking God for help, as his father had done, he went to his friends, who were young and foolish, and asked their advice. They appealed to his pride, telling him to show the people that he was better than Solomon by making them afraid. "My father made your burden heavy," Rehoboam told his subjects, "but I am more powerful than he was, and so I will make you work harder than ever. He had you punished, but I will set upon you with whips that are like stinging scorpions!"

When they heard this, all of the northern tribes of Israel rose up and went to their tents. "We have no future with this man," they said. "The House of David can look after itself from now on!" And they chose their own king, a man named Jeroboam, who had been bold in rebellion against Solomon. King Rehoboam was furious at this, and badly frightened. He sent his slave master out to punish them—Adoram, who was chief over all the forced labor in the land—but the people of the ten northern tribes set upon Adoram and stoned him to death. And at this, Rehoboam mounted his chariot in great haste and fled to Jerusalem.

From this time on for many, many years Israel was divided into two parts: the kingdom of the north, called Israel, and the kingdom of the south, called Judah. Only two tribes remained loyal to the House of David: the people of Judah and the Benjaminites. The seat of their power was the city of Zion, Jerusalem, that was often called now David's city. But so weak were they, once divided as a nation, that the Pharaoh of Egypt was able to send an army into Jerusalem at will, only five years after Solomon's death. And he took all the golden vessels from the Temple for himself, and all the golden shields that Solomon had made; and all of the city was in his power.

# Ahab and Elijah

After Solomon, there were nineteen kings of Israel, before the fall of the north, and nineteen kings of Judah before the fall of the south; and the worst of them all was Ahab. Ahab was the seventh king of Israel; and he was married to Princess Jezebel of Tyre, who hated the Lord and did her best to slaughter all of his prophets. During the reign of Ahab and Jezebel, many children were sacrificed to the abominable god Baal.

The greatest of the prophets in those days was Elijah. When he saw the wickedness of Ahab and Jezebel, Elijah told them, "By the God of Israel, there shall be a great drought now in this land; and no drop of rain shall fall without my order!" Then Elijah went to hide in the wilderness, and the Lord sent ravens with food for him to eat. For a long time, no rain fell.

"Go to the town of Zarephath, in Sidonia," God told Elijah, "a widow who lives there will feed you." So Elijah obeyed, and when he came to the widow's house, he asked for something to eat. "My son and I are nearly dead from starvation," the woman said. "I am sorry, but I have almost nothing to give you." "Do not be afraid. God will give us all that we need," the prophet told her. So she shared the very last of her bread with him, but when she looked again in her larder, there was plenty more. Elijah stayed on, and later healed her son miraculously when he appeared to be dead.

Meantime the crops of the northern kingdom were dying

for lack of rain, and Ahab had his soldiers out all over the country looking for Elijah. The prophet decided at last to go to the King. "So there you are, you scourge of Israel," said Ahab; but Elijah replied, "I am not the scourge of Israel—you are! Now tell the people to gather on Mount Carmel, and I will teach you something you need to know!"

So the whole nation gathered, and Elijah said, "How long are you people going to limp, first on one leg and then the other? If our Lord is God, serve him! If Baal is God, then worship him and be done with it." The people agreed then and there to a Contest of Gods on Mount Carmel. Two bulls were sacrificed, and prepared on two altars, one to the Lord and one to Baal. Then the followers of Baal danced wildly around their altar and prayed for fire to consume the sacrifice; but nothing happened. "Why don't you call a little louder?" said Elijah. "Maybe that idol of yours is busy, and he does not hear you!" But they went on praying all day, and still Baal sent no fire.

At last Elijah cried out, "O Lord, God of Abraham, Isaac and Israel, now let them know that you are God!" And upon that instant the fire of the Lord descended from heaven, and his sacrifice was consumed. "Your Lord is the only God!" cried all the people. At this, Elijah turned upon the prophets of Baal and killed every one of them. Then he said to Ahab, "Go home and celebrate. I think I hear rain!"

The sky grew dark and filled with clouds, and the rain fell in torrents. Ahab mounted his chariot and dashed away. But the hand of God was upon Elijah; and he tucked up his cloak and ran home faster than the chariot, all the way to Jezreel.

# The Story of Jonah

Once upon a time, there was a man named Jonah who had a quarrel with God. "Get up, Jonah," the Lord had said to him one day. "Go east to Nineveh and tell the people there to mend their wicked ways!" But Jonah did not want to do that; and so he boarded a ship going in the other direction, toward Tarshish.

They had not been sailing long before a great storm came up, and the sailors on the ship said, "Pray to your gods, everyone, or we will all be drowned!" Then they looked at Jonah, knowing that he was a fugitive, and they asked him, "Look here, what have you done?"

"I am sorry," he replied. "It is all my fault. I am running away from God, but of course, it was he who made the sea as well as the land. You had better throw me overboard."

"Do not blame us for this, Lord," said the sailors, and they threw Jonah into the water. But Jonah did not drown. Instead, God sent a great fish to swallow him up. Jonah slid down into the belly of the fish, where it was cold and dark, and there he lay for three days and three nights, terrified. "Here I am, Lord," he cried, "down in the belly of a fish, still praying to you, still praising your holy name!" And when the Lord heard this, he had mercy on Jonah and made the fish vomit him up again, onto dry land.

"Now do what I said and go to Nineveh!" said the Lord God; and this time Jonah went. He prophesied to the people there that they would be destroyed by God if they did not repent within forty days. At this, everyone in Nineveh, including the King, put on sackcloth and ashes. They mourned sincerely for their sins and prayed to the Lord night and day. Meantime, Jonah went outside the city and sat on a hillside waiting to see what would happen.

Nothing happened, and this made Jonah furious. "I knew you would forgive them!" he shouted at God. "That is why I did not want to come here in the first place. You are always forgiving people, and so I have gone to all this trouble for nothing!" But God only answered him gently, "Are you right to be so angry with me, Jonah?"

And as Jonah sat there sulking in the hot sun, the Lord made a little plant to grow up over his head and cheer him. Jonah greatly enjoyed the cooling shade. Then, the next day, God sent a worm to destroy the plant so that Jonah was left sitting in the blazing sun again, angrier than ever. "I might as well be dead," he said to himself. Then he heard the Lord saying to him, "Are you right to be so angry with me about that little plant, Jonah? I grew it for you; but I also made Nineveh, which is a very large city. Should I have no mercy on that fine, foolish place, where there are a hundred and twenty thousand people who do not know their right hand from their left hand— not to mention some very valuable cows?"

# Naboth's Vineyard

ow, Naboth of Jezreel had a vineyard beside King Ahab's palace, and the king wanted it for his own. But Naboth would not give away the land that was his inheritance, and he would not sell it either. So the king went home, and he sulked in his bed and would not eat.

"A fine king you are!" said his wife Jezebel. "I will get Naboth's vineyard for you!" So she wrote false letters saying that Naboth had cursed God and the king, and she sealed them up with Ahab's seal and sent them. The innocent man was convicted and stoned to death. "Take the vineyard now, if you wish," said Jezebel. "Naboth is dead!"

Ahab went down to claim the property, but the Lord told Elijah about it and sent him to the king. "You are a murderer!" said Elijah; and Ahab hung his head in shame. "You have found me out," he said. "Yes I have—and you are a thief as well. Now you and all your family will be destroyed," the prophet cried. "Where the dogs licked Naboth's blood, there they will lick yours; and the birds of the wilderness will eat the bodies of your children if the dogs do not. And because she has led you to do this, dogs will eat the body of your wife Jezebel in the field of Jezreel; for there has never been a king and a queen as wicked as you two!"

# Elijah and Elisha

When Jezebel heard what Elijah had done to the worshipers of Baal, she swore to hunt him down and slaughter him. Elijah fled again into the desert, with despair in his heart. "End my life, Lord," he prayed, "I am useless to you!" But God pitied him and sent angels to care for him; and the prophet made his way through the wilderness until he reached Mount Horeb. There, in the place where the Lord had spoken to Moses, Elijah rested, hidden away in a deep, dark cave.

God sent a great wind to his hiding place, and then he sent an earthquake and a fire. Elijah trembled and hid his face in his cloak. In the morning he went to the entrance of his cave and looked out. The dew lay sparkling on the slopes of the mighty mountain, and then, in a still, small voice God spoke to Elijah and said, "Go and anoint Elisha of Shaphat as my prophet to succeed you! It is he and the future monarch King Jehu who will punish the wicked in days to come; for I mean to spare only those of my people who have not given themselves body and soul to the worship of Baal!"

So Elijah journeyed on to the home of Elisha, and there he found his successor plowing with twelve oxen in a field. "Come with me," said the prophet, placing his cloak over Elisha's shoulders. And Elisha stopped only to say farewell to his parents; he left his farm and followed Elijah from that time on.

One day as they walked together near the river Jordan, Elijah asked, "What can I do for you, since I must soon leave this world?" Elisha answered boldly, "O Master, let me inherit a double portion of your spirit, if you must go." And the old prophet replied, "It may be so, if you see me as I depart." At that moment a chariot of fire appeared between them in the air, and a great whirlwind swept Elijah up into the sky. "O my father! O chariot of Israel!" Elisha cried, for he had seen it all.

And so Elisha went on to preach God's word and to perform many miracles. Under his guidance King Jehu was anointed and the House of Ahab brought to ruin; yet the

wicked Jezebel lived on. When Jehu came riding to her palace gates, she waited to test her powers against him, standing at her high window with her face painted and her body beautifully adorned.

Jehu looked up and saw her. *"Who is for me?"* he called to her servants. At this, they rose up and hurled Jezebel from her window, and the new king's horse trampled her bleeding flesh underfoot. Jehu entered the palace, and when he had eaten and drunk his fill, he told her servants, "Give Jezebel a decent burial, for, after all, she was the daughter of a king." But when they went out to the courtyard they could not find her. Nothing was left of Jezebel but her skull, her hands and her feet. The ancient prophecy of Elijah had come true: for he had said that someday dogs would eat the body of Jezebel in the field of Jezreel.

# Amos: The Angry Shepherd

The northern kingdom, Israel, grew prosperous now, and the rich began to trespass upon the rights of their neighbors. In fine new houses they lay upon couches of ivory with silken cushions, drinking wine, while the children of the poor went hungry. Baal was their god and the laws of the Lord were forgotten.

Then out of the south came Amos, a rough and simple shepherd filled with righteous anger and concern. At the shrine of Bethel he stood up boldly, saying, "Hear the word of the Lord, all you people! You betray the God who brought you out of Egypt." And he cried:

> Beware! I will send the Assyrians to defeat you!
> And you will be brought into exile for your sins.
> Far beyond Damascus I will send you;
> On the Day of the Lord the sun will go
>     down at noon
> And only a remnant of you will I rescue,
> As a shepherd saves from the hungry lion
> Only the broken limbs of the slaughtered lamb.

Amaziah, the priest at Bethel, was outraged. "Go home to Judah," he ordered Amos. "We want none of your mad threats and visions here!" But Amos replied, "It is the Lord who speaks; it is he who took me from my flocks and sent me to you." And until he was finally banished, Amos roamed the northern kingdom saying continually, "Woe to you who oppress the poor! The end is near; prepare to meet your God!"

# The Fall of the Northern Kingdom

The enemies of Israel, the kingdom of the north, and of Judah, the kingdom of the south, were pressing at all their borders, and still Israel and Judah would not cooperate. They chose this time, in fact, to fight more fiercely than ever among themselves; and when the armies of the north came down to besiege Jerusalem, King Ahaz of Judah was close to despair.

Now, one of the greatest of the prophets, a man named Isaiah, was a young man of noble family living in Jerusalem at this time, and Ahaz turned to him for advice. "Trust only in the Lord," Isaiah told him. "Above all, do not turn to the Assyrians for help. They are cruel enemies and they hate our God." But Ahaz was weak and afraid, and so he did exactly that. He went to the Assyrian leaders, bringing the riches of the holy Temple as gifts, and asked their protection in return.

The Assyrians were delighted. They helped themselves to the gold and silver, and they sent Ahaz home to make the Lord's Temple into a place more pleasing to their own gods. Then they attacked in the north. They captured the King of Israel and put him in chains. They dragged the people of the north from their fine homes and sent them away, far east of Damascus, to live the rest of their lives as exiles and refugees.

As a young man, the prophet Isaiah had been seized by the power of God in the Temple at Jerusalem. Standing there in prayer one day, he felt the earth shake beneath his feet; the great Temple filled with smoke and he saw the Lord God himself, seated on high with winged seraphim about him singing:

*Holy, holy, holy, Lord God of Hosts,*
*Heaven and earth are full of your glory!*

In joy and terror Isaiah cried out, "How can this happen to me, Lord, for I am only a sinful man among sinners, and my lips are unclean!" But when he had said this, a seraph came to him, bringing a glowing coal from the altar, and placed it upon his lips; and by the touch of that holy fire Isaiah was cleansed. Then he heard God saying, "Whom shall I send among the people to preach my word?" and Isaiah replied, "Lord, I will go. Send me!"

From that moment on, Isaiah gave himself into God's service. During all his long life he was a great teacher of the people and a counselor of kings. When he saw the weakness of King Ahaz, Isaiah knew that the Assyrian invaders would soon turn their full might against Jerusalem and that the city of Zion and the House of David would be in utmost peril.

It was then that the God of Israel came again to Isaiah, lifting up his heart so that it was as if he stood upon a high

# *Jerusalem*

mountain, gazing out upon the future of his people and seeing it all with clarity. Isaiah saw that the Assyrians would be given power to punish Judah, as well as Israel, for its sins; but he also saw that Assyria itself and many other enemies of the Israelites would be destroyed in time. Everything that happened on earth was part of God's carefully designed plan.

Truly there was great suffering ahead of them, Isaiah told the people. They had been selfish, faithless and false to God. Because of this, Jerusalem would be laid waste and they would be taken into exile far away. Only a few of them, a remnant, would be saved to return; yet they must never fall into despair. In a future time known only to God, a wonderful child would be born into the House of David: a wonderful Counselor, a Prince of Peace. His name would be Immanuel, which means "God is with us"; and during his rule, the Children of Israel would at last see righteousness and justice on earth. When this royal child is born, Isaiah said,

> *The people who have walked in darkness*
> *Shall see a great light.*
> *And the wolf shall lie down with the lamb;*
> *The calf and the lion shall feed together,*
> *And a little child shall lead them.*
> *There shall be no hurt, no harm*
> *On all this holy mountain;*

*Swords shall be hammered into plowshares,*
*Nation shall not rise up against nation,*
*And there shall be no more training for war:*
*For the earth shall be filled with the knowledge of God*
*As the waters fill the sea.*

During Isaiah's lifetime, the King of Assyria brought people from Babylon and many other foreigners to settle the captured lands of the northern kingdom; these people were called Samaritans, and they were regarded for years afterward as thieves and trespassers. King Ahaz died, and his son Hezekiah came to the throne in the south; and the old prophet Isaiah

lived on in Jerusalem. Closer and closer to the holy city came the armies of Assyria. Finally Sennacherib, the proud Assyrian king, sent his messengers to the very gates.

There they stood with a vast army behind them, and King Hezekiah went into the Temple of God to pray. "Look, Lord," he cried, "Sennacherib of Assyria mocks the living God! Here he is at the gates of your holy city! Save us, I beg you."

Soon he had a message from Isaiah saying, "The God of Israel tells me that he has heard your prayer, and has decided that the boastful Sennacherib shall not enter the city. He shall be taught who is in power here!"

That very night, the angel of the Lord went into the camp of the Assyrians and struck them down with a terrible plague; thousands of their men died on the spot. In the morning, Sennacherib had no choice but to go back home on the road by which he had come; but this was not the end of his punishment. Soon afterward, in his own country he was

worshiping at the temple of his Assyrian god and there he was approached by two of his own sons, who took out their swords and murdered him. So ended the life of the proud King of Assyria; and for a little while longer the people of Jerusalem were spared; and still the prophet Isaiah lived on.

# A Book Is Found

After the days of King Hezekiah the power of Assyria declined, but their false gods and foolish superstitions still held sway in Jerusalem. The Lord was recognized, yet his laws had been neglected so long that the people did not know how to obey them any more, or how to teach them to their children. Nevertheless, in the eighteenth year of his reign, a good-hearted king named Josiah, of Judah, sent workmen to repair the Lord's Temple; and while they were bringing fresh building materials into the holy places one day, the High Priest said to one of the king's servants, "Look what I have found!" The man looked, and said, "It is a book!" and he brought it to the king.

Josiah opened the book and began to read it; then he burst into tears. The more he read, the more he wept as if his heart would break. For this was the book of the Law of Moses; and here were the rules of the covenant with God that should have been obeyed all those many years.

"Come and hear this!" the king commanded. And he called them all before the Temple—prophets and priests, rich and poor, young and old—while he read aloud to them every word of the book of the Law. When he had finished, there was a great outcry among the people; and they all joined together in making fresh vows of love and loyalty to the God of Israel.

# Jeremiah and the Fall of Jerusalem

**I**t was a sad day for the people of Judah when King Josiah was killed, some years later, in a border skirmish with Egyptian troops. After his death they lost interest once more in God's holy laws; and now the city of Zion stood like a frail fort in the wilderness, surrounded by enemies. In the village of Anathoth, near Jerusalem, a boy named Jeremiah grew up knowing that his familiar world would very soon be destroyed, if not by the Egyptians or the Assyrians, then by the great Babylonian armies that were now gathering in the east.

Young Jeremiah stood watching the village potter work with clay. He saw the man deliberately breaking down a vessel that had turned out badly, and then he saw him using that same clay to make something else, far better. This, he thought, is what God intends for his people. He holds us in his hands; it is he who made us. But we have failed to obey his laws; therefore we must be broken down and later made anew.

And now the Lord spoke to Jeremiah, saying, "I formed you long before you were born, Jeremiah! I made you to be my prophet and to speak for me. Do not be afraid; I will tell you exactly what to say. Jerusalem will fall, yes. But in you my words will find an even stronger home, and thus they will live on."

Jeremiah went forth to preach, for he loved God more

than his own life. But, since he was a person who felt things very deeply, it was hard for him to give the people a message so full of desolation and doom. Unless they repented immediately, he told them, God would punish them with plague and sword. Long years of captivity lay ahead of them, in Babylon. And Jeremiah could see that they were in no mood to change their ways, for the wicked were rich and powerful in Jerusalem then; and they did not want to hear about their sins.

One cold day in the dark time of the year, King Jehoiakim, of Judah, was sitting in his winter palace at Jerusalem with a fire burning in a brazier before him; and his courtiers came to him in great alarm. They brought a scroll on which the words of Jeremiah's prophecies had been written down by a scribe named Baruch. "This man Jeremiah is dangerous!" the men told Jehoiakim. "He is saying that the King of Babylon is going to destroy this city and carry us all away into exile!" King Jehoiakim replied, "Well, let us hear it, then," and he sat listening with all of his guards and servants around him while the entire Book of Jeremiah was read aloud.

During it all, the expression on the king's face did not change. Without a word, he took up a knife and, as each section of the scroll was read, he cut it off and threw it into the fire. When the entire book had been destroyed, King Jehoiakim said quietly to his guards, "Arrest Jeremiah and Baruch!" But when the men went out into the city searching for the prophet and his scribe, they could not be found; for the Lord had hidden them away. Even now, in their place of concealment, Baruch was beginning to write down every word that Jeremiah told him, on a fresh scroll.

In the years that followed, Jeremiah was forced many times to go into hiding, and often he barely escaped with his life. Nebuchadnezzar, King of Babylon, came to the gates of Jerusalem with an immense army and placed the city under siege. In time the suffering of the people was so terrible that there was nothing for them to do but surrender and hope for the best.

Thousands of them were taken now into captivity in Babylon. Their rulers and their nobles were taken, and all the skilled workers and all the people of distinction in the city, together with their wives and all their children. The treasures of the Temple and the Palace were stripped away and carried off to Babylon. Jeremiah was imprisoned in Jerusalem; and when he continued even there to preach God's word, he was thrown into a deep well and left there to die. At the last moment, he was rescued by a palace servant who let down ropes and drew him out; but then he was put into prison again.

And this was not the end of Jeremiah's trials, or of the suffering of Jerusalem; for a few years later the people who remained mounted a rebellion against their Babylonian conquerors, and this time Nebuchadnezzar was determined to wipe Jerusalem from the face of the earth. He came back with his armies and killed or captured nearly every living soul who was left in Judah; and he burned down the Temple and destroyed the Ark of the Covenant, which had been carried throughout all the wanderings of the Israelites in ancient times. When he was finished, the city of Zion lay in ruins, utterly forlorn and desolate.

# By the Waters of Babylon

**I**t was a time of humiliation and terror for the surviving people of Judah. Men, women and children by the thousands had suffered torments during the siege; they had seen their holy places and their homes destroyed; and then they had been forced by their conquerors to march, half naked, frightened and ashamed, far away into the strange land of Babylon. At the time of Jerusalem's final ruin, their king had been Zedekiah. Nebuchadnezzar seized him, and, to punish him for rebelling, killed his sons before his eyes, and then blinded him and led him off in chains.

Most of the exiles were not treated so badly as this, but they were stunned by the loss of all that they held dear, and they were grief-stricken by the sense that the God of Israel had at last utterly abandoned them. Knowing that they had sinned, they wept, as they walked into exile, with remorse as well as pain.

"Come, let us have some merriment here!" cried the Babylonians, seeing tears on the faces of their prisoners. "Sing some of your quaint, old Hebrew hymns for us! You are in our power now, and we want to be amused." But at this, the hearts of the captive people blazed with fury, and they would not obey. Only among themselves did they continue to pray and sing and prophesy, and to dream both day and night of a time when they might be free once more.

# Consolation and Prophecy

The Children of Israel were scattered now like lost sheep over the landscape of the known world. Some fled to Egypt, forcing the old prophet Jeremiah to go with them against his will. But even while he had been in prison, and while Jerusalem itself had been besieged, Jeremiah had done an extraordinarily hopeful thing. He had bought a piece of land in Anathoth, the village of his childhood, where he and his blood relatives held ancient rights of inheritance. "Take the deed for this land," he had told Baruch in the presence of his guards, "and bury it deep, in an earthen pot. For the Lord has told me, *My people shall own fields and vineyards in this land again.*"

And before he left for Egypt, Jeremiah told the people who remained, "The Lord says: I am breaking you down now so that I may form you anew. When your buildings are all destroyed and your wealth is all gone, then I will make a new covenant with you; and I will put my laws deep within you, where they will live forever. From this time on, my words will be written not on a scroll or a tablet but upon your very hearts."

Jeremiah disappeared into Egypt, but he sent messages of comfort to the people in Babylon; and among themselves, over the long years of exile, they found new sources of hope and consolation. Jeremiah's understanding had been right: that the

people would survive even this punishment for their sins if they truly turned toward God once more. In a strange, flat land they labored for overlords whose habits seemed to them barbarian; they saw great wealth around them, and yet they came to know that the true riches of Israel were those of the mind, and of the soul.

One of the greatest of the prophets in exile was Ezekiel; to him a great many marvelous visions were given, and he taught them to the Israelites. It seemed to Ezekiel, one day, that he was carried away to a long, deep valley where he saw before him a vast number of dried and whitened bones. And God said to him, "These are the bones of my defeated people, lying here without hope. Tell me, son of man, can these bones live?" Ezekiel did not know how to reply; but then the Lord told him, "I am going to send the breath of life into these bones; and I shall put flesh and sinews upon them! For I am the Lord God, and I can do even this." As Ezekiel watched in wonder, the dead bones rose up and formed themselves anew into living bodies, and the host of Israel stood before him, shining and strong.

"God has shown me our future!" Ezekiel told the people. "Someday he will gather us from the ends of the earth and make one people of us again, Judah and Israel, strong among the nations. And from the House of David, he will raise up a great leader for us, a good and mighty Shepherd who will mend our wounds and find all those who have been lost. And he will lead us home again in peace, to the rich green pastures of our own beloved country."

# A Voice in
# the Wilderness

The people of Judah had lived in exile for many years by
now. Nebuchadnezzar's prisoners had seen their children
grow up in captivity, and their grandchildren, too. They had
worked in the fields and cities of their conquerors, longing
to be free; and they had prayed together year after year that the
Lord might bring them home to Jerusalem.

Hardship had taught the nation a purer view of what was important in life, and a greater sense of belonging to one another
and to their God. In time they came to feel that their suffering
might not be wasted, that it might have a purpose in God's plan
for his world.

Now a great new prophet appeared in Babylon. His name is
unknown, but he is called the Second Isaiah. "Comfort, O comfort you my people," the Lord God told him. "Prepare a way for
me in the wilderness, a broad highway! For soon the world will be
changed; and every valley will be lifted up, and every mountain
will be brought low. And all that is crooked now will be made
straight, and darkness will be made light; and all human beings
will gaze upon the glory of God!"

"What does he mean?" the people asked one another when
they heard the teachings of the new prophet. "Is God himself
coming down from heaven to save us?"

"He must mean Cyrus, the new Persian king," replied some of the Israelites. "Cyrus is going to conquer Babylon, and he is friendly to us, so he will set us free."

"Cyrus will trample the nations before him," said the prophet. "Like the rising sun he will come from the east, and he will take Babylon. Then we will go home at last, to build a New Jerusalem." The people cheered and wept for joy, and embraced one another.

"Do you not understand what that means?" the prophet asked them. "Do you not know yet? Listen: *Who made Cyrus? Who gave him his power? Who is it that rules over every nation, looking down at us as if we were dust, as if we were bubbles winking at the rim of a pail? Lift up your eyes and look at the stars! Who put them there? Who holds up the heavens like a tent for us to dwell in? What shall I cry?* I asked the Lord, and he told me,

> *Cry,*
> *All flesh is like the grass,*
> *Like a wildflower, it is beautiful,*
> *But the grass withers, and the flower fades,*
> *And the word of God lives on forever!*

"But will Israel be saved?" the people asked him. "Will King Cyrus come soon to set us free?"

"It is not enough for Israel to be saved," Isaiah told them. "Israel must be a light for all mankind. Our nation struggles and labors now, but we are like a woman in childbirth; our efforts have a purpose. It is through us that all the people of the earth shall be set free."

188

"How can that be, when we have no power at all?" asked the people, and the prophet told them,

Fear not, says the Lord,
My servant is my chosen one,
In whom my soul delights.
Although he is a man despised,
A man of pain and sorrow,
He shall be lifted up,
He shall be glorified,
Princes shall bow down to him,
And kings shall stand amazed.
Shout for joy, my people!
You shall hunger and thirst no more!
He who pities you will feed you,
He who cares for you will bring you
To living springs and to wells
In the wilderness.

"Who is the servant of God?" asked the people. "When will he show us the water in the wilderness?"

"Behold my life," said Isaiah. "Look at my ugliness, my poverty; look at your own suffering in captivity. We are a defeated people, yet God loves us as his own. He does not choose the proud and mighty to do the real work of his world. The servant of God comes to the grief-stricken knowing grief. Only because Israel has suffered can salvation come through us."

"But we are being punished unfairly," argued some of the younger people in the crowd. "It was our parents and grandparents who sinned against the Lord. Other prophets teach us that we must pay only for our own sins from now on. How can we save the world?"

Isaiah replied, "The Lord says,

> *The servant of God has not sinned,*
> *He is innocent.*
> *Like a lamb he is led to the slaughter;*
> *He does not protest.*
> *He suffers for the sins of others;*
> *By his wounds, the world is healed.*

"We do not understand this," said some of the Israelites. "Yet we are happy, for we see that God still loves us, and we know that soon we will be free." Others said, "Look! God must be using us as an example. He will make leaders of us now among all the other nations." But Isaiah said,

> *He will gather you into his arms*
> *Gently now as a shepherd takes his sheep.*
> *Rejoice, Israel!*
> *For the spirit of the Lord is upon me,*
> *And he has sent me to bring good news*
> *To the poor, he has anointed me*
> *To heal the brokenhearted,*
> *To preach freedom to all captives,*
> *To comfort all those who mourn.*
> *And soon you will depart from here in peace.*
> *Listen, listen to me and your souls will live!*
> *And you will go home again rejoicing,*
> *And the very hills will shout for happiness,*
> *And all the trees will clap their hands for joy!*

# Return to Jerusalem

Isaiah had prophesied it. King Cyrus of Persia captured Babylon, and the exiles were free to go. Not only this, but Cyrus proclaimed, "It is your Lord God who has given me this victory, and I intend to have a temple built for him in his own land. Therefore, people of Judah, go in peace and let all your neighbors give you gifts of gold and silver, cattle and other offerings from this country to your God who is in Jerusalem." Then Cyrus gave back the sacred vessels that had been stolen away from the Temple of the Lord fifty years before by Nebuchadnezzar, and a great company of exiles began the long, long journey home.

It was not easy, after so many years in Babylon, for many families to return to a place that their children had never seen, a place where no homes waited for them and no crops had been planted. For this reason, some remained in the land of their former captivity, keeping the ancient customs and remembering to pray to God among themselves. For the many thousands who returned, it was a time of joy mixed with sorrow. The land they so loved was desolate, and the great city of Zion lay in ruins without even a wall to protect it. The elders and priests set up an altar immediately, and made burnt offerings to the Lord; but it was many months before they were able to begin building a new temple. The Ark of the Covenant was gone forever; and on the day when the new foundations of the Temple had been laid, and the priests lifted up their trumpets and their cymbals in celebration, the people set up a cheer that was mixed with sounds of weeping. The elders among them remembered the glory of Solomon's Temple; and the sight of these new stones on the raw ground was almost too much to bear.

Some time later, at the Persian court, a man of Judah named Nehemiah worried about the plight of his countrymen. "Let me go and bring help to the city of my ancestors," he begged the king; and because the Persian monarch so greatly respected Nehemiah, he was sent to that region as governor.

On the night when Nehemiah arrived, he rode alone from gate to gate all around the broken walls of Jerusalem, pondering and planning. In the morning he said to the people, "Come! Let us bear this shame no longer! Let us begin rebuilding the walls!" The people took heart at his presence. Priests and merchants, shepherds and craftsmen together divided up the job and began to work, clearing away the rubble. Soon the beginning of a new city wall appeared.

"What are these ridiculous people doing?" jeered their rich, Samaritan neighbors in the north. "Don't they ever learn when they are defeated?" They gathered with other unfriendly tribes, meaning to attack Jerusalem. But the workers at the wall took up their weapons, and some stood guard while others quickly hauled stones; and some lifted stones with one hand, holding their weapons in the other. In fifty-two days the wall was finished, and no one dared to attack.

And so life began anew in Jerusalem, but there were troubles within the city as well as without. Many of the former exiles had married foreign women, and they had taken up Babylonian customs and even Babylonian names for themselves. They did not have their ancestors' sure sense of who they were and what their special relationship was to God.

One man who grieved deeply over this was Ezra. He had come back to Jerusalem determined to rebuild the strength of his countrymen as a holy people. "You have sinned in marrying these foreigners!" he told them. "You knew that was forbidden by our Law. You must send them away now, and all the children born to them." It was raining that day in Jerusalem, and the people stood trembling in the square before the Temple, while their tears mingled with the rain. "Give us time!" they begged. And they went away mourning and sorrowing; yet their loyalty to the Lord was so great that, in a few months' time, they had obeyed even this hard command.

Then the men and women who remained, and the children who were old enough to understand it, came together to study the book of God's Law. Ezra read it aloud to them during one long morning by the Water Gate, and when he had finished he said, "Jerusalem has its walls again, but it is God who is our true fortress; and our eternal stronghold is his holy Law. Wipe away your tears, for this is the feast of the Tabernacles!"

So the people of Jerusalem went out into the hills gathering branches of olive and pine, myrtle and palm, to make the booths they would live in for this feast; and for seven days and nights afterward they made merry and rejoiced.

# Job

There was once a man in the land of Uz called Job; and he was a true and noble man who had walked all his life in God's holy ways. Job had enormous numbers of herds and many servants, and he had fine sons and daughters, whom he dearly loved. Throughout the country, he was famous for his goodness, and much admired.

One day the angels of God gathered in heaven, and Satan came among them. "Where have you been?" the Lord asked Satan. "Oh, around the earth, hither and yon," the Devil replied. "Did you notice my servant Job?" asked the Lord. "There is a good man!"

"He is good because you make it easy for him," said Satan. "Take away his rewards and he will curse your name."

"Very well," said the Lord. "Take them away and we shall see. But you must not touch Job himself." So Satan went to work.

The next day, messenger after messenger came to Job with horrifying news. All of his livestock had been carried off by robbers. His wealth was gone, and every one of his beloved children had been killed. Stunned by grief, Job fell to the ground; but instead of cursing God, he said, "The Lord gives and the Lord takes away. Blessed be the name of the Lord."

Then Satan went back to heaven and said to the Lord, "That

was not much of a test. You would not let me touch him! But if his flesh is hurt, then I know he will curse you." The Lord replied, "Try him, then, but you must spare his life." So Satan put terrible, open sores all over Job's body, and he was a man in torture day and night. Still he did not curse God.

Now, at this time people believed that pain and sickness were punishments for sin, and word went out that Job must have done something terrible. His neighbors began to despise Job and to make fun of him, and he was so hideous by now that even his own wife did not like to come near him. But three old friends of his decided that they should come and give him some good advice. When they arrived and saw Job in his agony, they were so overcome by horror that for seven days and seven nights they sat beside him without speaking a single word. Finally, Job broke the silence; but he did not curse God; instead, he cursed the day that he had been born, and railed against his fate.

Eliphaz of Teman answered him first, saying, "Do not complain, Job! You have brought this on yourself. Ask God what you have done wrong, and he will forgive you."

"I have done nothing wrong!" cried Job. "You do not understand my suffering! The worst of it is that I cannot go to God and demand a fair trial, for I do not know how to reach him."

"Those are shocking words," said the second man, Bildad of Shuah. "You should not argue with God, you should beg his forgiveness. All men are sinners; you ought to know that."

"I know as much about God as you do!" roared Job. "Stop tormenting me! God made me the way I am. He must know that I am innocent. But how could I have a fair trial if he is the one who is against me, and he is also the judge?"

"Control these wicked thoughts!" said the third man, Zophar of Naamath. "Beware the wrath of God and mend your ways."

"Listen, *listen* to me!" shouted Job. "You can do nothing else to help me now; at least do that! I am innocent!" And he went on to argue his case with God as if he were in court; but his three friends scorned him, and they went away.

Indeed, Job's behavior had been spotless. So perfect a man was he that he would have won his case in any ordinary, human court of law. But when he had finished speaking, something far more wonderful than that happened to him. The Lord God Almighty in all his glory came to Job, and spoke to him. "Stand up, little Job!" God said. "I am here. I know you, but you do not know me. How could you? Where were you when I laid the foundations of the earth, when the morning stars sang together? Were you in charge? Do you know how to make a world?" Then God took up the suffering man into the heart of the whirlwind, and he let him see all of Creation. For a long moment, Job lost his own small life within that tremendous vision. He understood that undeserved suffering is only one of life's great mysteries; and his soul rejoiced, because at last he had seen his God.

"I burn with anger against you!" the Lord said to Job's friends. "Your preaching was mean and stupid. You understand nothing at all!" The three men hung their heads in shame. But to Job, God gave back perfect health, and also gave him splendid sons and daughters and twice as much wealth as he had ever had before. And Job lived on after that, a long and happy life.

# The Story of Esther

This is the story of Esther, who risked her life to save her people when they were in exile. Nebuchadnezzar had captured Esther's family, and she lived with her foster father, Mordecai, under the Persian rule, for King Xerxes had taken Babylon. Because she was very beautiful, Esther was invited with many other young women to serve at court, and when Xerxes had taken notice of her, he became so enchanted that he made her his bride.

One day, Mordecai learned of a plot in the realm. He sent word of it secretly through Esther so that the king was able to save himself from traitors; yet he did not know who his champion had been. Therefore he made no move to help Mordecai when, soon afterward, Mordecai himself was in grave danger.

What had happened was this. Mordecai was proud of his heritage as a Jew—that is, a man of Judah—in this foreign land; and so he refused to bow down and prostrate himself upon the ground when the king's chancellor passed by. At this, Haman, the chancellor, was furious. "I will destroy this man Mordecai," he vowed. "More than that, I will destroy his people, too!" He went to the king about it. "That is your business," said Xerxes. "Do what you like." So Haman sent out orders all over the country that the Jews were to be slaughtered, every one. Then he had a scaffold built, on which to hang Mordecai.

No one at court knew that Queen Esther was Mordecai's cousin as well as his adopted daughter. High in her royal chambers, she wept for her foster father and all her people, and shook with fear. If she said nothing, she knew she might live on in royal luxury and honor, safe from all harm. If she revealed herself, and even if she tried to reason with this proud, impetuous king, she would almost certainly be killed.

Nevertheless, dressing herself in all her royal splendor, Esther approached the throne. Before she could speak, Xerxes said to her, "I have just discovered that it was Mordecai who once saved my life! I have decreed that Haman shall hang upon his own scaffold, and Mordecai shall be given all of his wealth and power. Now, what is it that you want, my dear?"

Again Esther might have remained silent. Her father was safe, and she might have turned her back upon her people. Instead she stood up boldly before all the court and said, "O King, if I have found favor in your sight, grant me one request!" And the king replied, "I will give you anything, even half of my kingdom." Esther said then, "Spare my people, and give me my own life, for I am also a Jew!"

The king held out his golden scepter and granted her wish. Quickly, messengers were sent throughout the land with a proclamation that the people of Judah were not to be killed. Instead, they were given royal permission to strike back at all of their enemies. Queen Esther herself decreed the day of triumph, which was celebrated then for the first time, and which became known as the feast of Purim.

# The Fiery Furnace

In the days when Nebuchadnezzar ruled in Babylon, there was a young man from Judah named Daniel who was chosen, together with three of his fellow exiles, to be trained as a companion to the king. Willingly they studied all that they were taught about literature, history, and the wisdom of the ages; but Daniel said, "We must keep the Law of God! Therefore we must not defile ourselves with food from the king's table." And with the help of the Lord, the four boys grew strong without drinking anything except water and without eating anything but vegetables.

When it came time for them to serve at court, Nebuchadnezzar found the young men ten times wiser than all the magicians and sorcerers in his kingdom; and he discovered that Daniel had a marvelous ability to understand dreams. Nebuchadnezzar was a troubled monarch, and he came to count upon Daniel's help in explaining the frightening visions that floated into his mind while he was sleeping.

One day the king had a tremendous golden statue set up in the land of Babylon, and he gave orders that everyone without exception must fall upon the ground at a signal and worship it. Now, the three companions of Daniel, whose names were Shadrach, Meshach, and Abednego, were discovered refusing to do this; and when they were threatened with torture they still refused, for they would worship no power but the Lord God. The king was outraged. "Throw them into the fiery furnace," he said, "and make it seven times hotter than usual!" So Shadrach, Meshach, and Abednego were bound and cast into the flames to die a terrible death. But when the king's servants looked in later, expecting to see nothing but charred bones, instead they saw three men walking freely about. They were not burnt at all, or even charred; and with them in the furnace walked a fourth figure, who was a guardian angel of God. "It is the Lord who has saved them!" cried Nebuchadnezzar. "Set them free, for theirs is a God of great power!"

After this, the dreams of Nebuchadnezzar tormented him more than ever. "I heard a mighty voice!" he cried one day to Daniel. "What does it mean? There was a great tree whose top reached the sky, and the birds from heaven nested in its branches. But the watchers and the holy ones came down, and one said, *Cut down this tree; destroy it utterly! He shall go like a beast into the fields and eat grass, until he learns that God Almighty rules over the kings of the world!*" And Daniel told the king, "I am sorry, but it means that all of this must happen to you unless you stop thinking that you are all-powerful. For it is God who has given you your kingship, and he can take it away from you at any moment. Give praise to the King of Heaven, for his ways are just and he has power to humble those who walk in pride!"

But Nebuchadnezzar did not give up his proud ways. "Look at this wonderful city of Babylon!" he was saying one day. "It is I who built it!" At that moment the Lord struck him down in a madness that sent him raving into the fields. And after that, the great king ate grass like a beast, and wandered alone in the wilderness.

# Belshazzar's Feast

After Nebuchadnezzar in Babylon, Belshazzar was king, and he was as proud as his father had been. One night he gave a great feast and had his food served in the holy vessels that had been stolen from the Lord's Temple, in Jerusalem. In the midst of the revelry, as the great hall was ringing with shouts of mirth and drunken laughter, Belshazzar suddenly turned pale and began to shake with terror. There, on the palace wall beside him, was a human hand without a

body, it was writing these words: *Mene, mene, tekel, upharsin.*

"What does this mean?" shrieked the king. But no one could explain it, and so Daniel was brought into the hall. There, before all the astonished and terrified people, he told Belshazzar: "It means that you have not learned your father's lesson. You have worshiped gods of gold and silver, and you insult the God of Heaven by using his sacred vessels in this way. The hand that writes is from God, and the handwriting says: You have been judged and found wicked; your kingdom is taken now by the Persians!"

Indeed it was that very same night that Belshazzar was struck down and murdered by his enemies; and Darius the Persian came with his armies and conquered Babylon.

# Daniel and the Living God

One after another, during the long years of Daniel's exile, the kings of Babylon fell; still he lived on to prophesy and preach. Many visions came to him in which the usual boundaries of time and space were not present, so that he could perceive the larger patterns of God's intent. Often Daniel conversed with angels, and looked upon their shining faces, and heard their mighty voices in his mind.

In one of his visions, Daniel saw the kingdoms of the earth in the form of four great beasts. Each one in turn held power, but in the end they were all destroyed. Then came the Lord's Day of Judgment, which was the end of all things past and present; and after this, Daniel said, "I saw coming in a cloud from heaven, one like a son of man. And to him were given all power and all glory; for his is a rule over all times and all places. He shall be monarch of all people, and his kingdom shall last forever and ever!"

By such visions as these, Daniel was amazed and shaken. It was hard for him to live in such a way and also continue with his appointed tasks in the Babylonian court. Still, he wrote them all down faithfully and kept them sealed in a safe place. Meantime, King Darius trusted and respected Daniel so deeply that he put him in charge of one hundred and twenty chiefs of his kingdom.

Soon the other leaders became jealous of Daniel and searched for a way to destroy him.

In a body, they came to the king one day and said, "You know the penalty for traitors, your Majesty! They must be thrown into the lions' den to die. Now, Persian law states that we must worship only you; yet Daniel falls upon his knees three times a day, facing Jerusalem, and it is to the Lord God that he is praying. Will you obey the law?" King Darius was heartbroken, for he loved Daniel; yet he knew that he must send him to the lions' den, where people were torn to pieces for their crimes. He had no choice; he signed Daniel's death warrant, and then he went to his own apartments to fast and pray.

At morning's first light the sleepless king rose and went to the lions' den. In anguish he called out, "Daniel, Daniel, servant of the living God, are you still alive?" Then he saw Daniel, standing quietly in the pit among the lions. Hungry as they were, they had not touched him all through the night, because he had trusted with all his heart and soul that his God would save him.

So Daniel was restored to his high office, and his enemies were punished. Then Darius wrote a proclamation to all the people of his great empire, saying:

> *Peace be with you!*
> *Let all nations honor the God of Daniel,*
> *Who has saved him even from the lions:*
> *For this is the Almighty, the living God,*
> *And his kingdom shall have no end.*

# Psalms

**P**eople of all ages, and of many faiths and nations, have turned to the Psalms, for here we find the most powerful of emotions known to human beings: joy and wonder, grief and anger, terror and despair, adoration of the sublime. Some of these beautiful songs and hymns were written by King David. Others came to us from unknown poets, telling and retelling over the years the great moments of a people's close and passionate relationship with their God.

Here are some lines from the King James Version of the Bible, brought together here so as to remind us of the story we have read thus far. In praise of the creation of the world, and of man and woman, the psalmist sings:

*The heavens declare the glory of God;*
*And the firmament sheweth his handiwork. . . .*     PSALM 19
*The day is thine, the night also is thine:*
*Thou hast prepared the light and the sun.*
*Thou hast set all the borders of the earth. . . .*     PSALM 74
*. . . marvellous are thy works. . . . I will praise thee;*
*For I am fearfully and wonderfully made.*
*Whither shall I go from thy spirit? . . .*
*If I take the wings of the morning,*
*And dwell in the uttermost parts of the sea;*
*Even there . . . thy right hand shall hold me.*     PSALM 139

A wandering people upon the earth, the Israelites lived always intimately with God. Again and again he came to them, offering his covenants, leading them out of the wildernesses of the body and of the soul, teaching them his holy Law:

*The waters saw thee, O God, the waters saw thee. . . .*
*The voice of thy thunder was in the heaven;*
*The lightnings lightened the world. . . .*
*Thou leddest thy people like a flock by the hand of Moses. . . .*

PSALM 77

*When Israel went out of Egypt. . . .*
*The sea saw it, and fled. . . .*
*The mountains skipped like rams. . . .*
*Tremble, thou earth, at the presence of the Lord,*
*At the presence of the God of Jacob.*          PSALM 114
*With my whole heart have I sought thee:*
*O let me not wander from thy commandments! . . .*
*I am a stranger in the earth. . . .*
*Give me understanding, and I shall keep thy law.*   PSALM 119

Battling for possession of the Promised Land, they perceived it as a holy war and begged the Lord to help them:

*Surely thou wilt slay the wicked, O God. . . .*
*Do not I hate them, O Lord, that hate thee? . . .*
*I hate them with perfect hatred. . . .*          PSALM 139
*Let burning coals fall upon them:*
*Let them be cast into the fire;*
*Into deep pits, that they rise not up again.*       PSALM 140

At last the young nation dwelled in a land of its own and built a great city:

212

*Behold, how good and how pleasant it is*
*For brethren to dwell together in unity!*
*It is like the precious ointment upon the head,*
*That ran down upon the beard, even Aaron's beard:*
*That went down to the skirts of his garments. . . .*  PSALM 133
*Praise the Lord; for the Lord is good. . . .*
*For the Lord hath chosen Jacob unto himself,*
*And Israel for his peculiar treasure.*  PSALM 135

Their days of glory were soon over. Unfaithfulness to God's commandments, selfishness, and pride helped to bring about the ruin of the beloved city, and a captive people mourned:

*By the rivers of Babylon,*
*There we sat down, yea, we wept,*
*When we remembered Zion.*  PSALM 137
*Out of the depths have I cried unto thee, O Lord.*  PSALM 130
*My God, my God, why hast thou forsaken me?. . .*
*Our fathers trusted in thee: they trusted,*
*And thou didst deliver them.*
*All they that see me laugh me to scorn. . . .*
*I am poured out like water. . . .*
*My heart is like wax; it is melted. . . .*
*. . . O Lord: O my strength,*
*Be not far from me . . . for there is none to help . . .*  PSALM 22

But in their anguish, God did not abandon them. Even to the bitterness of defeat and exile, he brought them the sweetest of comforts, the most profound of all consolations:

*The Lord is my shepherd; I shall not want.*
*He maketh me to lie down in green pastures:*

*He leadeth me beside the still waters.*
*He restoreth my soul: he leadeth me*
*In the paths of righteousness for his name's sake.*
*Yea, though I walk through the valley*
*Of the shadow of death, I will fear no evil:*
*For thou art with me; thy rod and thy staff*
*They comfort me. Thou preparest a table before me*
*In the presence of mine enemies;*
*Thou anointest my head with oil;*
*My cup runneth over.*
*Surely goodness and mercy shall follow me*
*All the days of my life:*
*And I will dwell in the house of the Lord for ever.*     PSALM 23

Returning once more to their homes, the people met with many discouragements; still they were gladdened by the presence of God:

*. . . he gathereth together the outcasts of Israel.*
*He healeth the broken in heart,*
*And bindeth up their wounds. . . .*     PSALM 147
*Therefore will not we fear,*
*Though the earth be removed, and though the mountains*
*Be carried into the midst of the sea. . . .*
*There is a river, the streams whereof*
*Shall make glad the city of God,*
*The holy place of the tabernacles of the most High. . . .*
*Come, behold the works of the Lord. . . .*
*He maketh wars to cease unto the end of the earth; . . .*

He breaketh the bow, and cutteth the spear in sunder.

He burneth the chariot in the fire. PSALM 46

And they looked forward to a day when he might be revealed to
all nations:

Be still, and know that I am God:

I will be exalted among the heathen,

I will be exalted in the earth. PSALM 46

Praise ye the Lord. Sing unto the Lord a new song. . . .

PSALM 149

Praise ye the Lord. Praise God in his sanctuary, . . .

Praise him with the sound of the trumpet. . . .

Praise him with the timbrel and dance. . . .

Let every thing that hath breath praise the Lord.

Praise ye the Lord! PSALM 150

# Between the Old Testament and the New

O n a hilltop in northern Greece stood a boy of eighteen with a great, black stallion. Together they looked out over the vast plains that stretched before them to the curve of the blue horizon. "With a horse such as this," thought the boy, "I could leap the space before me and challenge the sun god in his lair!" The stallion tossed his head and stamped. "Soon, Bucephalus!" said the boy. "Soon we will be on our way, and I will tell you what we are going to do. We are going to conquer the world!"

The boy was Alexander, son of King Philip of Macedon, pupil of the great philosopher Aristotle; and his dream came true. Nineteen when he first commanded his father's cavalry, Alexander died only fourteen years later, far from home, in Babylon. But in that brief time Bucephalus had borne his master to the very edges of the known world; kingdom after kingdom had fallen to the military genius of the young warrior-prince; and nations far to the south and to the east of Alexander's birthplace had come to know the rule, the customs, the architecture, and the beliefs of the Greek people.

One of the many countries conquered by Alexander the Great was Persia; another was Egypt; and a third was the little land of Judah, whose capital was Jerusalem. Upon Alexander's death his empire was divided among three of his generals, who soon began to quarrel among themselves; and once again the city of David, with its new Temple and reconstructed walls, became a battleground. As these hard years passed, the people of Jerusalem found to their sorrow that the new ways of their Greek and Syrian rulers caused even more harm to them than fire or sword. Zeus and Apollo, the gods of the Greeks, were supposed to be worshiped now; a scandalous Greek gymnasium was built in the holy city; and the ancient religious customs of the Jews were despised. Women and children were tortured for obedience to the Mosaic Law; sacred books were burned; and some of the people of Judah became so discouraged that they turned away from their covenant with God. For so many years their prophets had promised them a great new leader, a Messiah from the House of David, who would bring about the kingdom of God on earth; yet nothing of the sort had happened, and by now they did not know what to think.

The darkest day of all came when King Antiochus Epiphanes entered the holy Temple and placed there, above their altar, the "abomination of desolation," which was the symbol of the god Zeus. At the sight of it, so great was the fury of the people that they found new and desperate courage. At the same time, a young man who was to become their hero and liberator was growing up in the north. This was Judas Maccabeus, a youth of great charm and power, bold in his leadership as David had been, and fiercely loyal to his heritage.

Judas Maccabeus was one of five brothers, all sons of a man named Mattathias, who had come from Jerusalem to live quietly

in the village of Modein. One day when Judas was a young man, the soldiers of the King came to his village and tried to force the people to make sacrifices to Zeus. They wanted Mattathias, especially, to bow down before the Greek god, for he was a respected leader there. "You have five fine sons," they said to him. "We will reward them well if you obey!"

But as Judas Maccabeus stood watching, his father stepped boldly forward and said before the crowd, "If every nation on earth and every other person alive stoops to worship this vile image, my sons and I will not!" Then he took out his sword and killed the king's deputy on the spot and tore down the pagan altar. After this, Mattathias and his sons fled into the hills, leaving all their possessions behind them.

The little band of rebels was soon joined by other Jewish patriots known as the Hasidim, and then numbers of refugees came to help them make up a small army. In the mountain passes and in the desert they continually raided the forces of the king, causing Antiochus great concern. When his father died, Judas Maccabeus became their leader, and now they began to win some major victories.

"We must annihilate these people!" cried Apollonius, the king's commissioner. He brought in a vast army of mercenaries from Samaria, but Judas routed them and seized the great sword of Apollonius for his own. For the rest of his life he kept this mighty weapon at his side, and with it led his men to victory. "Do not be afraid of their numbers!" he told his people. "The God of Abraham is with us; he will lend us his strength!" An even larger army was sent now by the king. Six soldiers marched down upon every one of the rebels; yet they fought so fiercely that they slaughtered the enemy forces and marched in triumph to Jerusalem.

Tears streamed down the faces of the sturdy warriors when they saw their Temple standing in ruins, with weeds growing tall among the tumbled stones. It had been desecrated by the tyrants, and now it must be cleansed. They set about their work, and soon, with fresh incense and a new altar, it was ready for holy sacrifices once more. The candles were lighted and, for eight days, the people of Jerusalem celebrated the first feast of Lights, which was to be remembered ever afterward as Hanukkah.

Still, more hardship was to come upon the small and troubled land. Out of the west now came a new kind of army, tremendously well equipped and well organized, with warriors and magistrates who brought with them yet another set of foreign ways and pagan gods. These were the forces of Rome. They were friendly to Judah at first, yet in the long run they were determined to rule all other peoples of the world according to their own laws.

In Egypt, a queen named Cleopatra played her wit and beauty against the power of two of these Roman rulers. In Jerusalem, leaders from the west and from the east battled one another until Judah, too, became a Roman province, with a governor named Herod. What would happen now to all the hopes and dreams of Abraham's descendants, the people who looked to the book of Law and the holy Temple as the central power in their daily life? What would happen to those who still waited faithfully for the House of David to bring them a Messiah, a kingdom, and peace on earth?

# THE NEW TESTAMENT

# Time of Miracles

In the beginning, when God made heaven and earth, he said, "Let there be light!" and there was light. And the light that streamed forth into darkness was part of his being, and it was a power that helped him to shape the world.

And there came a time when this same light was born into the world as a human child, because God loves his world and every human being. As he grew up, God's child was a light to the world, a light by which we can see truth. And his life was a saving way for us through the world's darkness, a way by which all of us may become children of God.

For many years the prophets had told of his coming; and now in the land of Judah, during the rule of Herod, it was time at last for the Savior's earthly life to begin. So it was that the angel Gabriel came one day to the home of a young woman of Nazareth whose name was Mary.

"Hail, favored one!" said the angel. "The Lord is with you." Mary was troubled at first by his presence, but Gabriel told her, "Fear not, Mary, for you are blessed among women. And you shall give birth to a son, and his name shall be Jesus. To him the Lord God will give the throne of David, and he shall be a great king, who shall reign forever."

"How can this happen?" asked Mary. "I am only a young girl, living apart from any man." And the angel replied, "Nothing is impossible for God. The power of the Holy Spirit will come upon you and cause the child to be born; therefore he shall be called the Son of God." Mary bowed her head. "I live to serve the Lord," she said. "Let it be as you have told me."

When the angel had departed, Mary rose up and went quickly into the hill country to visit her cousin Elizabeth. For many years Elizabeth had grieved because she was barren; and now, to their astonishment, she and her husband had found that she was having a baby, late in her old age.

Mary came to the door of her cousin's house and called out to her. At the sound of Mary's voice, Elizabeth felt a great stirring of the life within her, and her mind was suddenly ablaze, at the same moment, with an understanding of all that had happened. With a loud cry she ran to Mary, saying, "Blessed are you among women! And blessed am I, for today I am visited by the mother of my God!" The two women embraced, and this was Mary's song of joy:

> *My heart exults in the Lord,*
> *For he has regarded his lowly handmaiden. . . .*
> *He humbles the proud and the mighty,*
> *He comforts the barren and raises up the poor. . . .*
> *Now in his mercy he keeps his promise to Israel,*
> *To Abraham, and his people forever and ever!*

And Elizabeth said, "I was sure of it as soon as you spoke, and my unborn babe leapt for joy. This child of mine is a blessing indeed; but it is yours who will be the Lord and Savior of us all!"

# The Child Is Born

From the birth of Abraham to the birth of David there were fourteen generations; and from David to the Babylonian exile there were fourteen more; and from the exile to the birth of Jesus there were another fourteen. But when Mary came to live with her promised husband, Joseph, who was of the House of David, she was already with child. Not knowing that her baby came from God, Joseph was troubled, and he decided that he should send her away. He planned to do this quietly, for he was a kind person and he did not wish to shame her. However, the angel of the Lord came to him in a dream, saying, "Do not hesitate to marry this young woman, for she carries the Son of God, who is coming to save people from their sins." When he had heard this, Joseph took Mary as his wife and cared for her with great tenderness.

And in those days a decree went out from Caesar Augustus, the Roman emperor, that all people should be taxed and that each should go to be enrolled in his own city. So Joseph went from Nazareth, in Galilee, to Bethlehem; and Mary came with him, heavy with child. When they arrived after the long, hard journey, they found that there was no room for them at the inn.

Where could they stay? Mary was so tired. And then they realized that her time had come; the baby would be born that very night. Into the stable of the inn they went at last, where there was straw to rest upon and the warmth of the farm animals quietly breathing all around them. And there in the stable Mary gave birth to her child; and she wrapped him in swaddling cloths and laid him in a manger.

Now, in that part of the country there were shepherds out in the fields, keeping watch over their flocks by night. And an angel of the Lord appeared to them, and the glory of the Lord shone around them, and they were very much afraid. But the angel said to them, "Fear not, for I bring you good news! A great joy comes now to all people, for this day in Bethlehem a Savior is born who is Christ the Lord. This is how you will find him: He is wrapped in swaddling cloths, lying in a manger." And suddenly there was with the angel a great gathering of the heavenly host saying, "Glory to God in the highest; peace on earth to all people of good will!"

When the angels had gone away into heaven, the shepherds looked at one another in astonishment. For so long their people, and all their ancestors before them, had awaited the arrival of a mighty prince. Could he have come to them tonight, here in their own village, to dwell among plain folk like themselves? "Let us go over to Bethlehem," said one of the shepherds. "Yes," said the others, "let us go and see."

So they rose up quickly and hurried to the nearby town; and there they found Joseph and Mary in the stable, and they saw the newborn baby in the manger. "It is the holy child of God!" they whispered to one another. And then they said to Mary and Joseph, "We were in the fields, and the angel came and told us." As the new day dawned, Mary heard the shepherds going about the town, calling out to everyone the news that Christ the King was born; but she kept all that had happened quietly in her heart, and pondered it.

Soon afterward there came to Jerusalem wise men from the east, who said to King Herod, "Where is the child who has been born King of the Jews? For we have seen his star in our own lands, and we want to worship him." At this, the king was filled with jealousy and fear. "One prophet has said, *Look for him in Bethlehem*," Herod told them. "But if you find him, let me know." King Herod had a plan.

So the wise men took the road south out of Jerusalem, and, to their great joy, the star they had seen earlier went on before them, until it came to rest over the place where Jesus was.

Dressed in their fine boots and jewels, and their cloaks of silk, the wise men stepped down from their camels, into the stable yard. Then they entered the stable and saw Mary with her son. Down upon their knees they fell, and worshiped him; and they brought out the rich treasures they had brought for him: gold, and frankincense, and myrrh.

Before the wise men left Bethlehem, they were warned in a dream not to tell Herod what they had found. So they returned to their homes by another way, without going into Jerusalem. A few weeks later, Mary and Joseph did travel to the Holy City; for Jesus was circumcised on the eighth day and, according to the Law of Moses, there must be a ceremony of purification at the Temple, in Jerusalem, thirty-two days after that.

Now, at this time in Jerusalem there lived an old man named Simeon who was very wise and much beloved by God for his holiness. And the Lord had told him that he would not die until he had seen his Savior with his own eyes. As soon as Mary and Joseph entered the Temple to offer the praises and sacrifices that were proper for a firstborn son, Simeon strode through the crowd directly to them and reached out and took the baby in his arms. "Thanks be to God!" he cried. "It has happened at last! Now, Lord, let your servant depart in peace; for I have seen Israel's salvation; I have looked upon the child who shall be a light to all nations!" Then he turned to Mary and said, "Through your son many shall fall and rise, and much that is hidden shall be revealed; and a sword shall pierce through your own soul, also."

Mary and Joseph were filled with wonder at all this, but they went back quietly to Bethlehem. In the meantime, King Herod was growing more and more furious. It was clear that the three wise men had tricked him. He decided to wait no longer before taking action. "Go to Bethlehem," he told his soldiers. "Since we do not know which is the newborn king, you must kill every male child born in the past two years. Spare not one!"

The soldiers obeyed him. Throughout the region there was a terrible shedding of innocent blood, and everywhere the desolation of mothers who could not be consoled, crying for their babies. But the angel of the Lord had warned Joseph in a dream, and he had wakened Mary in time to escape. Quickly they took up the baby Jesus and fled with him by night to the land of Egypt, far away.

# Boy in the Temple

When they heard that Herod was dead, Mary and Joseph brought Jesus back to Nazareth. By now he was a young boy, growing tall and strong. Every year he went with them to Jerusalem for Passover; and when he was twelve years old, Mary and Joseph looked for him after the feast but discovered that they could not find him. They had been traveling north from Jerusalem in a great company of friends and relatives, and they did not realize that Jesus was missing until the end of the first day's journey on crowded, dusty roads.

They turned back immediately and began searching for Jesus throughout the city, but without success. Mary was badly frightened by the time they came to the Temple, on the third day; and they went inside and discovered that, indeed, there he was. All around young Jesus sat the elders and the rabbis of the Temple, watching him and listening to him, amazed at his intelligence. Whenever he answered one of their questions, they gazed at one another with eyes inquiring, *Who is this child?*

"Why have you done this to us, my son?" Mary asked. "We have been so worried! We have been looking everywhere for you." And Jesus calmly answered her, "Mother, you should have known that I must be here, in my Father's house."

# John the Baptist

For many months Elizabeth's husband, Zechariah, had not spoken a word. The angel of the Lord had come to him in an overwhelming vision, saying that a child would be born to him, a great and gifted son named John; and from that moment on, the astonished old man had been unable to speak.

The time came at last for the baby to be born, and Elizabeth brought forth a fine, strong son. "What will you name him?" their friends and relatives asked. "John," she replied. "Why John?" they wondered. "No one in this family has ever been named John." Then they turned to Zechariah. "What name will you choose for your son?" they asked him. Zechariah, still mute, took out a tablet and wrote upon it, "His name is John." And immediately, to everyone's amazement, he regained his power of speech. "Blessed is the God of Israel!" he cried. "This is the child who shall go before the Most High, preparing his way."

Years passed, and the child became a strange and solitary young man. Into the wilderness of Judea he wandered, and there, like Elijah the prophet before him, he fed on locusts and wild honey; and like Elijah he wore a garment made of camel's hair, with a leather belt about his waist. "Come to the river," he told his countrymen. "Come and be baptized in the Jordan, so that you may be cleansed of your sins." Seeing that he was a man

of God and a prophet, people in great numbers came to John, and after he had baptized them, many stayed on to learn his holy ways. "What shall we do now?" they asked him; and he said, "You must change your lives. Stop robbing and harming others! Share what you have and show kindness from now on!"

"Are you the Christ who has come to save us?" some people asked. "No," replied John the Baptist, "I am not. The Lord is so much greater than I that I am not worthy to untie his sandals. I am the one prophesied by Isaiah, sent to tell you that your darkness will soon be made light. I baptize you with water for repentance's sake, but, sinners, beware! He will baptize you with the flame of the Holy Spirit when he arrives."

And then, one day, among the crowds of people beside the Jordan there came a man from Galilee quietly walking alone. At the edge of the river he stopped for a time; and then he called out to John, asking to be baptized. At the sound of his voice, John leapt up. Quickly he ran to his new visitor; and after they had stood for only a moment face to face, John said, "Lord, it is you who should baptize me." But Jesus answered gently, "Do what is fitting at the present time, John."

And thus the Son of God was baptized. As he rose from the brown, brackish waters of the river Jordan, he looked up at the sky. Above him he saw the heavens opening, and then the Holy Spirit descending to him in the form of a dove. Then he heard a voice from on high, saying, "You are my beloved Son, in whom I am well pleased."

# Temptation

As soon as he had been baptized, Jesus went away alone into the desert to fast and pray, and the devil came after him. Forty days and forty nights later, Jesus was very hungry, and the devil said to him, "Look at all these fine, round stones on the ground here! If you are the son of God, why don't you turn them into bread and eat all you want?"

But Jesus answered, "It is written in holy Scripture that *Man does not live by bread alone, but by every word that comes from God";* and he refused.

Now the devil took Jesus to Jerusalem and lifted him to the highest ledge of the Temple. "If you really are the son of God," the devil said, "throw yourself down from here and see what happens, for it is written in Scripture that *Angels will save you.*" But Jesus answered, "It is also written that *You shall not tempt the Lord your God";* and he refused.

Finally the devil carried Jesus to a great mountaintop and showed him all the kingdoms of the world. "I will give you everything you see now, and power over all of it," the devil said, "if only you will bow down and worship me." But Jesus answered, "It is written, *I am the Lord and you must have no other God but me!*"

When the devil saw that Jesus could not be lured by any sort of temptation, he went away; and angels came to Jesus and comforted him.

# Lamb of God

Who was that man?" John's disciples asked him after they had seen him baptizing Jesus. "The time of waiting is over," said John. "I have seen the Holy Spirit come down to greet him. He is our Messiah, he is the Christ." Then, as they stood talking together, they looked up and saw Jesus nearby, walking beside the river. "Behold the lamb of God, who takes away the sins of the world!" said John.

Hearing this, two of the men began to walk down the path after Jesus, and when he had noticed them he turned and looked intently at them. "What are you seeking?" he asked. At first they did not know how to reply, and so the man named Andrew asked him, "Master, where do you dwell?"

"Come and see," said Jesus.

The men followed him, and after they had spent several hours talking with Jesus, Andrew went to his brother and said, "We have found the Christ!" Then he took his brother to meet Jesus, and Jesus looked at him and said, "So you are Simon, the son of John! From now on, your name shall be *Peter*."

The following day, Jesus decided to go up to Galilee. There he met a man named Philip, and he said to Philip, "Follow me!" Immediately, Philip rose up and followed Jesus; and soon after this, Philip went to his friend Nathaniel, who came from the same place as Andrew and Simon Peter. He said to Nathaniel, "We

have found the leader who was promised to us by Moses and the prophets. His name is Jesus of Nazareth."

"Nazareth!" said Nathaniel. "Can anything good come out of that place?"

"Come and see," answered Philip.

So Nathaniel went with Philip, and when Jesus noticed him drawing near, he said, "Look! An Israelite who is an honest man!" Nathaniel's eyes opened wide. "How did you know me?" he asked Jesus. And Jesus replied, "I saw you before Philip called to you, when you were sitting under the fig tree." Nathaniel was amazed. "Under the fig tree! But that was at a distance, much earlier! How could you have seen that? Master, you are the Son of God! You are the King of Israel!"

"You believe that," said Jesus, "simply because I said, 'I saw you sitting under the fig tree!' Come now, Nathaniel, you shall see far greater things than that. Truly, I tell you that you shall see heaven opening, and angels going up to God and coming down again to greet the Son of Man."

On the next day there was a wedding in the town of Cana, in Galilee. Jesus was invited to the wedding, together with his followers; and his mother, Mary, was there also. Friends and neighbors from all over the countryside had come together for this joyous celebration, and the bridegroom's house was filled with people dancing and singing, all dressed in their finest; and everyone was feasting and drinking toasts in honor of the bride and groom. After several hours had passed, when the merriment of the crowd was at its height, Mary noticed that the bridegroom's servants were looking dismayed. The wine was all used up, and they had not a drop more to offer the guests.

When Mary saw what had happened she went to Jesus and whispered, "They have no more wine." Her eyes pleaded with him, but Jesus looked back at her as if she were a stranger. "What has that to do with me? My time has not yet come," he answered, and turned away. Nevertheless, Mary went to the servants and said to them privately, "Whatever my son Jesus tells you, be sure to do it."

A few moments later, Jesus came to the place where their host kept great stone jars for the water that was used, according to the Mosaic Law, for purification. Each jar was large enough to hold twenty or thirty gallons. "Fill these jars with water," Jesus told the servants, and they did. "Now draw some out and take it to the master of ceremonies," Jesus said. The servants obeyed. The water had been turned into splendid, fragrant wine, and the master of ceremonies tasted it. "This is magnificent!" he cried. Then, not knowing where it came from, he said to the bridegroom, "You have done something extraordinary! Most people offer their finest wine first, and save the poorer stuff for later. But you have saved the best for the last!"

Very few people knew what had really happened at the marriage feast, but some of Jesus' followers had seen it, and they believed in him. And this was the first miracle that he did.

# The Fishermen

On the shores of the Sea of Galilee, the sons of Zebedee sat in their father's boat, mending nets. Lately, James and John noticed, a quiet man had walked among them, looking often for long hours over the lake. Evidently he was a man of prayer, perhaps a man of some special holiness. Andrew and Simon knew him. His name was Jesus.

Sudden storms often swept these waters, and so the two brothers studied the wind and weather with great care. Each day, they had to catch fish or go hungry. The tools of their trade were as cautiously guarded as their own lives. This morning, they thought, it would be fair; and as the wind was rising, they saw Jesus coming toward them, accompanied by Andrew and his brother. They were going on a journey together, it seemed. Perhaps the holy man had come to say good-bye.

Jesus drew near and smiled at James and John. Then he said to them, "Follow me, and I will make you fishers of men!" When he was certain that they had heard him, Jesus turned and began striding down the path away from the lake, without looking back. Andrew and Peter went with him; and then, leaving their nets half mended, James and John rose to their feet and followed him too.

# Stranger in His Own Land

**J**esus went now to a town on the northern shore of the lake called Capernaum. The land was barren and marshy there, and the people suffered greatly from the heat in summer and from terrible infestations of mosquitoes and flies. Of all the people in Galilee these were the poorest of the poor; and many of them were ill in body and spirit as well. "I bring you good news!" Jesus told them. "The kingdom of God is here!"

Laying his hands upon the sick people, Jesus cured them one by one; and soon all the people in that region wanted to come and touch him, to receive the power that came forth from him and have their diseases cured. The sick who could not walk were carried to Jesus, and people whose minds were tormented by demons were also brought to him.

One sabbath day when he was teaching in the synagogue at Capernaum, a man there cried out in a loud voice that was not his own but the voice of the demon that possessed him. "What are you doing here, Jesus of Nazareth?" the demon asked. "Have you come to destroy us all? We know who you are! You are the Son of God!" And Jesus said, "Be still, speak no more! Come out of him!" And at this, the devil left the man, and he was healed.

Soon the fame of Jesus spread throughout the district, and he knew he must move on. But first he would stop for a time in Nazareth, where he had lived as a boy.

On the sabbath day in Nazareth, Jesus went with his old friends and neighbors to worship at the synagogue. When it was time for the Scriptures to be read aloud, he was given the Book of Isaiah, and he stood and read from it the words saying:

> The spirit of the Lord is upon me,
> And he has sent me to bring good news
> To the poor, he has anointed me
> To heal the brokenhearted,
> To preach freedom to all captives,
> To comfort all those who mourn. . . .

And when he had finished, Jesus said, "This day, here before you, the prophecy of Isaiah is fulfilled."

"Is he claiming to be the Messiah?" the people of Nazareth asked. "Nonsense! This is outrageous! We have known him since he was a child. He is the carpenter's son!"

"A prophet is not without honor, except in his own country," Jesus replied. Then he began teaching them, not as one who recites a lesson but as a person in authority. The longer he spoke, the more people stared and whispered. "Where has Joseph's boy got all this knowledge?" they asked. "How dare he speak to us in this way?" But Jesus continued calmly, telling them that if they did not believe in him they could not be healed and he would bring his ministry elsewhere. The murmur of the crowd became a roar of fury; and the people rose and forced Jesus from the building. Some were so angry they would have murdered him, but he escaped and made his way back to Capernaum.

# My Father's House

**S**oon it was Passover time, and Jesus went up to Jerusalem. Pilgrims were gathering from all parts of the country, bound for the magnificent Temple which stood at the heart of the Holy City. There they would offer the sacrifices and coins of tribute to God that were ordained by ancient Jewish law; and they would give thanks to God for his protection of their ancestors when they had fled from Egypt in days of old.

Jesus passed beneath the shining gateway of the Temple and entered the coolness of the inner courts. Once again he saw the place where he had stood as a child, talking with the priests and elders while his family searched the streets for him. That had been after another Passover feast, some twenty years before.

All around him now he saw sly and crafty merchants promoting overpriced wares: pigeons, sheep, and oxen for the people's sacrifices. Booths were everywhere, and greed was on every face. "Buy your local tribute coins from me, I'll give you a fair price!" shouted the money changers, laughing among themselves as they robbed and cheated the visitors. It was a loud and cruel scene, enough to sicken anyone who loved the house of God and the meaning of this holy day. Jesus was furious.

He made a whip, and with it he attacked the money changers. He turned over their tables and poured out their golden coins upon the floor. Then he stormed through the inner courts, driving before him all the commercial people and their creatures. "You shall not make my Father's house into a den of thieves!" he cried. The merchants fled, and the onlookers, shaken and curious, gathered around Jesus to hear him speak.

He spoke to them of the kingdom of God, and of the Temple. Gold has no value, he told them, unless it is used in God's service. Temples themselves can be broken down, and built again. What is sacred is the power that God gives us to be cleansed and live our lives anew.

Now, in Jerusalem at this time there were powerful people among the Jews called Pharisees and Sadducees; and when Jesus spoke of a new life, one of the Pharisee leaders, a man called Nicodemus, was troubled. Soon after this, Nicodemus came through the streets alone and in secret one night, to the place where Jesus was staying. "Master, I see that you are a teacher who comes from God," he said. "Tell me how a person can have a new life; for I was born once from my mother, and I do not understand how this can happen again."

"Truly, I tell you there is more to life than this," said Jesus. "When your body is born, that is flesh brought forth from flesh, but you also have a spirit. How can it be born? It must be brought to life by the water of baptism and the flame of the Holy Spirit, which comes from God. What is spirit? You cannot see it. It is like the wind; it goes where it wants to go; and that is what your freedom will feel like to you when you serve God and only God."

# The Woman at the Well

After the Passover, Jesus traveled north again with his disciples. Taking the shorter route into Galilee, they went through Samaria, although this was a country despised and avoided by most Jews. The journey was a tiring one. When they came to a place called Sychar, where there was an ancient oasis called Jacob's Well, Jesus stopped to rest and sent the disciples into the village to buy some food.

As he sat alone by the well, a Samaritan woman drew near to fetch some water. "Give me a drink," Jesus said to her. And the woman replied, "You are a Jew, and you ask me—a Samaritan—for a drink! I find that hard to believe!"

Jesus smiled at her. "If you knew what is being offered to you, and who is offering it," he said, "you would be asking me for a drink. And I would give it to you. I would give you the living water that comes from God."

The Samaritan woman began to laugh. "Are you a better man than Jacob?" she asked. "This was his well, and it is deep. You have no bucket! How will you get this living water of yours?"

And Jesus said to her, "If you drink from this well, you will soon be thirsty again. But if you drink the water I can give you, you will always be satisfied; for it will become a spring within you, welling up into eternal life."

"I want some of that," said the woman. "I am tired of carry-

ing my bucket here every day!"

"Then, go and call your husband. Bring him here," Jesus told her. "I have no husband," the woman said.

Jesus laughed. "You are right to say that you have no husband. You have had five husbands, and the man you live with now is not your husband."

The woman stared at him and began to tremble. "Who are you?" she asked. "You must be a prophet! But even in Samaria, we are waiting for the Messiah who is called the Christ."

"I am he," said Jesus.

Just then the disciples drew near, bringing food from the village, and paused for a moment in their surprise at seeing Jesus talking with a woman. When they saw her leaving, they approached Jesus and said, "Master, you should eat something!" But he answered them, "I have food you do not know."

"Has someone brought you food?" they asked.

"I am fed by the work that I do," said Jesus. "Doing the will of the One who sent me—that is my food!"

Meanwhile the woman had run back to the village, breathless with excitement. "The Messiah has come!" she cried. "He is there by the well! He just told me everything I have ever done!"

The people of the village begged Jesus to stay with them after this. And so for two days he visited the Samaritans, and in this time they came to believe in him, not because of what the woman had said but because they could see for themselves that he was the Savior of the world.

# The Sermon
# on the Mount

When Jesus returned to Galilee, a crowd of people quickly gathered around him, and so he went to the top of a small hill and sat there to speak. The faces around him were filled with the hopes and fears that have been felt by all human beings since the world began. With tenderness and understanding he looked upon each one, and this is what he taught that day:

Blessed are the humble-minded,
for theirs is the kingdom of heaven.
Blessed are the gentle,
for they shall inherit the earth.
Blessed are those who mourn,
for they shall be comforted.
Blessed are those who hunger and thirst for what is right;
they shall be satisfied.
Blessed are the merciful,
for they shall receive mercy.
Blessed are the pure in heart,
for they shall see God.
Blessed are the peacemakers,
for they shall be called God's children.

*Blessed are those who are persecuted for doing what is right; theirs is the kingdom of heaven.*

And then he told the ones who wanted to follow him: You must live good lives, for you are very precious to God; you are the salt of the earth. With you he will preserve his treasures; without you, how can he season anything? You are his salt, and you are also the light of his world. Now, when you light a lamp, you do not hide it under a bucket; you lift it to a high place where it can give light to all your house. In the same way, let your life stand high and shining in the world, so that all may see your good works and give praise to your heavenly Father for them.

"Do not think that I have come to destroy the Law," he told them. "I have not; I have come to fulfill it. But I tell you, it is not enough for you simply to go by the rules, as the scribes and the Pharisees do. You must do better than this, or you will never be able to enter the kingdom.

"In former days, people were taught: *You shall not kill.* That law is right, and it must never be changed, but it is not enough. I tell you that you must not even say hateful things about your brother, or hold a grudge in your mind against him. You must go and make peace with him, and be reconciled.

"And in former days you were taught: *You shall hate your enemy.* And it was said, *If one of you harms another, you must see to it that he is punished, an eye for an eye, a tooth for a tooth.* But I say to you now, You must do good to those who abuse you. You must love your enemy! For if you love only people who are kind to you, that says nothing good about your character. Any sinner can do the same! You must do something far greater if you are going to be like our heavenly Father, for he sends his sun to rise upon good and evil people alike, and he makes it rain upon the just and the unjust.

"Now, when you pray, do not show off about it. Do not heap up fancy words and phrases, for your Father in heaven already knows what you need. Go privately into your room, and simply say to him:

> *Our Father in heaven,*
> *Holy is your name.*
> *Your kingdom come,*
> *Your will be done*
> *On earth as in heaven.*
> *Give us today our daily bread*
> *And forgive us our sins*
> *As we forgive those who sin against us.*
> *Save us from the time of trial*
> *And deliver us from evil.*

And when you fast, do not go about looking dismal, as hypocrites do! They have their reward. But do your fasting in secret, for God knows all about you, and he will give you his reward.

"Where your treasure is," said Jesus, "there your heart will be also. Therefore do not store up possessions for yourself; they will only rot and rust, and a thief may steal them. Store up the riches of the spirit instead. Do not be anxious about your lives, constantly wondering, Will I have enough to eat? What shall I wear? Look at the birds of the air! They have no hoards or stockpiles, yet the heavenly Father provides for them. Look at the lilies of the field: They do not rush about collecting gold and fine garments; yet King Solomon in all his glory was not clothed more beautifully. Your Father in heaven knows what you need. If you put your energy into doing what is right, he will provide for you; and if you seek his kingdom first and foremost, many other things will be yours as well."

"We want only the kingdom! We are not greedy like the others," said some of the people listening to Jesus.

"Judge not, lest you be judged!" Jesus told them. "Why is it that you can always see the speck of wood in your neighbor's eye, but you never notice the log in your own? Hypocrite! First clean out your own eye, and then you may see well enough to help your neighbor with his. Treat him as you would have him treat you! But this has already been taught to you, by the Law and the Prophets."

"How many of us will enter the kingdom?" asked the people. "Will it be many, or a few?"

"The gate is narrow and the way is hard," Jesus said. "If you seek God on a wide and easy path, you will not find him. But if you go trustingly to his door and knock, will he not let you in? If your child was hungry and asked for bread, which one of you would give him a stone? And yet you are sinners; God has far more loving-kindness to offer than any of you.

"Seek and you shall find; ask and you shall receive. Yet, in days to come, beware of false prophets, for there will be many who are wolves in sheep's clothing. How will you know them? As a tree is known by its fruit. The good teacher brings forth treasures

from his heart's abundance, and good deeds are the result. No matter what his disguise, an evil person does what is wrong.

"But every person who hears my words and acts upon them shall be like the man who built his house upon a rock. When the storm comes, and the flood rises, then your house shall stand firm and safe, because it has a good foundation. The foolish man builds his house on sand, and the wind and the rain wash it away, and the house falls in ruins. Do not be like the foolish man! And do not come running to me later, crying, 'Lord! Lord!' and thinking that will get you into heaven, for it will not. Instead, go now and do the will of my Father, who sent me. That is the way to eternal life."

And when he had finished speaking, the crowds stood silent in astonishment, for Jesus spoke not like the scribes but as one in authority.

# A Storm Is Stilled

On the shores of the Sea of Galilee a boat was waiting, as a great crowd of people came clamoring after Jesus to the water's edge. He stepped into the boat and asked to be taken across the lake to the other side; and his disciples pushed their way through the crowd to accompany him.

The wind was rising, and the bright sky of early evening soon grew dark with storm clouds; but Jesus lay down in the boat with a cushion under his head and went to sleep. Wilder and wilder grew the waves, while the bow of the boat rose and plunged continually. At last, water began pouring over the sides of the little vessel and it appeared that it might sink; and still Jesus slept. The disciples awakened him, crying out in terror, "Master! Master! Save us! Do you not care that we are all about to die?" Jesus opened his eyes and looked out at the storm. Then he arose and exclaimed to the wind and the sea, "Peace! Be still!" Immediately, a great calm descended upon the lake from shore to shore. He turned to the disciples and said, "O men of little faith, why were you afraid?"

The trembling disciples looked away and did not know how to answer him; but each one wondered in his heart, "What sort of man is this, when even the winds and the sea obey him?"

# Healer of Galilee

**P**ressing close to hear his words and to receive his healing touch, people filled the little house where Jesus was staying in Capernaum, and overflowed into the yard beyond. Now four more men arrived, carrying a fifth, who was paralyzed and lying on a mat. The four men quickly saw that it would be impossible for them to bring their friend through the crowd, but instead of turning back, they climbed up on the roof of the house and cut an opening there. Then they lifted the sick man over the heads of the people and lowered him down on his mat to the place where Jesus was seated inside. Jesus was delighted by this, and seeing that it had been done because of their enormous faith in him, he said to the paralyzed man, "My son, your sins are forgiven!"

Now, some Pharisees and scribes were in the room watching all this, and they whispered to one another, "Who is this man? It is blasphemy for him to say such a thing! Only God can forgive sins." But Jesus told them, "The Son of Man has that authority." And he said to the paralyzed man, "Take up your mat and walk!" Immediately, the man rose to his feet, perfectly well, and walked away. "God be praised!" the people cried. "We have never seen anything like this before!"

Wherever Jesus went, he sat down to eat with the common people of the town and with the sinners, and even with the tax collectors, who were the most despised of all officials. The Pharisees were outraged. "Why does your master keep such company?" they asked the disciples. Jesus answered them: "I have come to save sinners. It is sick people who need the physician, not those who are well." Then the Pharisees said, "Why do you go about eating and drinking while we deny ourselves and the followers of John the Baptist are told to fast?" Jesus replied, "What fools you are! When John taught fasting, you said he must be mad. Now I eat and drink, and you call me a glutton. Truly I tell you, while I am here it is a time of rejoicing. My people are feasting now with me because I am their bridegroom; later they will fast."

While he was speaking with them in this way, a ruler of the synagogue named Jairus came to Jesus and fell upon his knees. "My little daughter is at the point of death! Come and lay your hands upon her, I beg you, so that she may live!" he cried. Jesus rose and began making his way through the immense crowd toward the home of Jairus; and in the crowd was a woman who had been suffering from a flow of blood for twelve years. No physician had been able to help her. When she saw Jesus, she thought, "If I can touch even his garment as he passes by, then I will be well." And she came up behind him in the crowd and touched his robe. Immediately the flow of blood stopped, and she was healed.

But Jesus perceived that power had gone forth from him, and he turned and asked, "Who touched me?" His disciples said to him, "With this crowd crushing us all, you ask, *Who touched me?*" Then the woman kneeled before Jesus in fear and trem-

bling, and confessed what had happened. "Daughter, your faith has made you well," said Jesus. "Go in peace."

At this moment, a member of Jairus' household drew near, saying, "The child is dead; we need not bother the Master." But Jesus said to Jairus, "Do not be afraid, only believe!" And he went into the house, where there was already a great tumult of weeping and mourning for the girl, who was only twelve years old. "What is all this noise?" asked Jesus. "She is not dead, she is only sleeping."

At first they laughed at him; but he made them all leave the house, and he went into the child's room with her mother and father and three of his disciples. Taking her by the hand, he said to her, "*Talitha, qumi!*" which means, "Little girl, arise!" And immediately she came to life again, and stood up and walked. "Give her something to eat," said Jesus, "and say nothing of this to anyone." The people were overcome with amazement, and although Jesus wanted his works of healing to be quietly received, the news of them continued to spread.

Sometimes Jesus went away by himself to pray; and sometimes he preached to great crowds of people by the sea, and sometimes in the synagogues. One sabbath day in a synagogue, the scribes and the Pharisees were watching him closely, for they had noticed a man among them who had a withered hand. Would Jesus dare to heal him on the sabbath, a day on which no work should be done? But Jesus knew what they were thinking. "Come here and stand beside me!" he told the man with the withered hand. Then he asked the people, "Is it lawful on the sabbath to do good or to do harm, to save life or to destroy it?" No one could answer him. "Stretch out your hand!" he told the man, and he did; and immediately his hand was healed. The Pharisees were furious, and they discussed among themselves what they might do to Jesus. But he said to the people, "The sabbath was made for man, not man for the sabbath."

From all over the country now, people came to Galilee to be with Jesus, saying that he was the long-awaited Savior of the Jews. Then, one day, a Roman centurion came to Jesus in great distress; and he was one of the soldiers who occupied the land of Israel at that time. "Master," he said, "it would not be right for you to come into my house, and I understand that, but I beg you to heal my servant, who is dying. Now, I am a man in authority myself, so I know what it is to give orders and have them obeyed. Only say the word, and I know that my servant will live." Jesus was deeply moved by this request. He said to his followers, "Truly, I have not found such faith among my own countrymen! I tell you, God's kingdom will bring grief to many people, for when his will is done, some who are now among the first shall be last, and some of the last shall be first." Then to the centurion he said, "You have believed it; so it shall be done." The soldier returned to his home, and found that his servant had been healed at the very time when Jesus said this.

And then, as he continued to speak to the people, a man came to tell Jesus that his mother and brothers were waiting outside to see him. "Who is my mother?" Jesus asked. "Who are my brothers?" Then, stretching out his arms to the people who followed him, he said, "These are my people, this is my family! My mother and my brothers and my sisters are those who do the will of God!"

# Seeds and Treasures

In the kingdom of heaven, Jesus taught, we are all one family and God is the Father of us all. When he spoke of the kingdom, he often used parables, and it delighted him that children were able to understand them, sometimes even better than their elders, for parables are stories designed to help people grow. They are stories with secret messages hidden inside them, and although they may look very simple, like seeds they are packed with possibilities, waiting for a good place to take root.

"The kingdom of heaven is like a mustard seed," he said one day. "Now, this is the smallest of all the seeds on earth, and yet when it is planted, it grows into the largest of shrubs. And still it continues to grow, putting forth large branches until it becomes a tree; and finally it becomes a tree so great that the birds of the air can come and build their nests in it. And that is what the kingdom of heaven is like. See this, if you have eyes to see!"

When Jesus told this parable, he was sitting in a boat by the shore, because so many people had followed him that he might have been crushed if he had tried to stand on the beach. And after this, he told another parable:

"The kingdom of heaven is like a treasure," he said, "that is hidden in a field. And one day a man comes walking through the field, and he finds it. What will he do? He will cover it up quickly to hide it again, and he will go to the town and sell everything that he has, so that he can buy that field with the treasure in it."

And again Jesus told a parable, saying, "The kingdom of heaven is like a great pearl, more magnificent than any other jewel that is on earth. When the merchant of jewels sees it, what will he do? He will go and sell all of his other stock, and everything he owns, so that he may buy that one great pearl at any price."

"What does he mean?" the people asked one another. "Is he saying that we must sell everything we own, before we may enter God's kingdom?" Jesus saw that they did not understand him, and so he told them one more parable that day:

"Once there was a farmer who went out to his field to plant some grain, and as he sowed the seeds, some fell upon a path where the earth was hard-packed, and the birds came along and ate them. Other seeds fell upon rocky ground and quickly began to grow; but their roots were so shallow that they soon withered away. Some of the other seeds fell among thistles, and as they grew up, they were choked to death by those tough, thorny plants beside them. But the last group of seeds fell on good soil and grew well; and they brought forth a rich harvest for the farmer."

When he had finished this parable, Jesus said, "He who has ears to hear it, let him hear." And he left the boat by the shore and went back to the house where he was staying. His disciples came hurrying after him. "We cannot understand that story, Master," they said to him. "What is the meaning of it?"

"If you do not understand that one," said Jesus, "how are you going to understand any of my parables? Listen: The seed is the word of God, and it needs good soil to grow in, for the

building of the kingdom. If it falls upon a hard place like the path, then it has fallen upon the deaf ears of hardhearted people; and the devil soon comes along and devours it.

"If it falls in a rocky place where the soil is not deep, and begins to grow, and then withers under the sun, then that plant is like the person who is glad at first to hear the good news about the kingdom; but having no inner strength of his own to offer, he soon forgets all about it and lets it die.

"The seed that falls among thorns is the one that is destroyed by the cares of this world. For the thistles growing up beside it are ambition and anxiety and the overwhelming desire for riches and material things, and these are the weeds that kill the growth of a person's spirit.

"But the plant that grows up tall and strong, the way it is meant to do, is the one that is rooted deep in the patience of a good and honest heart. This is the plant that puts forth its blades, and then its ripening grain, until it is finally a great and abundant harvest for the farmer, who is our heavenly Father.

"It is the same with my words, for my teaching is not mine; it comes from the Father, who sent me. So, the people who understand what I say, and live their lives accordingly, are the ones who will grow and produce—each in keeping with the very best of his ability—a harvest that is pleasing to God."

# Twelve Are Chosen

Now, as more and more people came to Jesus, he saw that they were like a great harvest that lies ripening in the fields without workers to gather it. And he was troubled about this, and so he went up into the hills alone and spent the whole of a night in prayer.

When the sun rose, he called twelve men to come to him, and these were Peter (who had been named Simon at birth) and his brother Andrew, James and John the sons of Zebedee, Philip, Bartholomew, Thomas, Thaddeus, Matthew (who had been a tax collector until he met Jesus), Simon who was called the Zealot, James the son of Alphaeus, and the disciple named Judas Iscariot.

Jesus explained to the twelve that they would now become his apostles, to help him carry on his ministry. "The people of Israel are like lost sheep," he told them. "Go and be good shepherds to them. Heal them and cast out demons, for I will give you this power. Bring them the news that God's kingdom is at hand; and teach them to live according to his will."

Their lives would not be easy, Jesus warned them. Leaving their families behind, they must travel from place to place, as he himself did, without having any home. They must take no money with them, nor extra clothing; nor should they ask any fee for their services, since their powers were freely given to them.

"When you come to a village," Jesus said, "seek out an honorable person and go to his door, saying, 'Peace be in this house!' If you are welcomed, accept the food and drink that are set before you, for the worker deserves his keep; and if you find good people there, share your peace with them; but if they are evil, let your peace return to you."

The faces of the twelve apostles were bright with joy and eagerness as Jesus told them all of this, but he looked at them tenderly, knowing of all the trouble and hardship they would have to endure. "I am sending you forth like lambs among wolves!" he exclaimed. "You will enter some towns and be badly treated by the people there, and they will not listen to your words. When this happens, leave that town and shake the dust of it from

your feet. Truly I tell you, it will be worse for that place later on than it was for Sodom and Gomorrah when devastation struck!

"You will be beaten in synagogues, and you will be arrested. Even your friends and your families will betray you, and some of you will be put to death. Still you must not be afraid. Be wise as serpents, innocent as doves; and do not worry what to say when you stand before kings and governors; the Holy Spirit will give you words. God cares for every sparrow that falls! How much more will he care for you, since you do this for my sake? The person who values his life must give of it freely; and whoever gives up his life in my name, though he may die for it, will win life eternal. Do not look back! Take up your cross, and follow me!"

# Death of a Martyr

**W**ho is this man called Jesus?" asked Herod Antipas, the Roman ruler of Galilee. "Can it be that he is the prophet Elijah back from the dead? Bring him here! I want to talk with him."

"Some say he is John the Baptist, risen again," Herod's courtiers whispered to him; and at this, the king grew pale and silent, remembering what he had done.

It had been a scene of splendor and of horror, at Herod's birthday feast at the palace. Herod and his queen had joined in celebration with his courtiers and all the leading men of Galilee, but even so, the king had not felt easy in his mind, for John the Baptist was in prison; and try as he might, Herod could not stop thinking about that fiercely righteous and holy man.

He himself had given the order for John's arrest. In part, this had been a trick to keep him safe from Queen Herodias, for she hated the Baptist and constantly searched for a way to murder him. John had been preaching repentance throughout Galilee, and everywhere he went, even into the court itself, he denounced Herod for his sin: Herod had taken his brother's wife, Herodias, and married her.

But there was another reason, as well, for the imprisonment. Herod was a weak and curious man who wanted John close by so that he could argue with him. Fascinated by the man's

courage, and by the boldness of the truths he continued to utter even within prison walls, Herod was drawn again and again to visit his captive. As time went by, he came away from these meetings ever more troubled and perplexed.

Then, on the night of the banquet, the beautiful young Salome, daughter of Herodias, had taken up her beads, her bells, and her veils, and she had performed an exquisite dance before all the company. It was late in the evening, and wine flowed freely, and Herod found himself overcome by Salome's charms. In his grandest manner, he proclaimed to her before all his guests, "Ask me for any reward, my dear! I will give anything in homage to such beauty, even half my kingdom!"

"What shall I ask?" the girl whispered to her mother. "Ask for the head of John the Baptist on a platter!" hissed Herodias. And so Salome said to the king, "I want the head of John the Baptist brought to me on a platter, at once!"

The king was deeply shaken. But he had made his offer, and before such a company he did not dare to retract it. He sent a guard to the prison, and while the revels continued in the great hall, the head of John the Baptist was struck off. The guard brought this terrible tribute back on a platter and presented it, as he had been ordered, to Salome. *What else could I have done?* the king asked himself now, shuddering at the memory. Slowly the girl crossed the hall and laid the platter before her mother. Herodias looked down at it and smiled. And the king knew now that as long as he might live, he would never be able to forget that smile.

# The Pool of Bethesda

**I**n Jerusalem there was a place of healing called the Pool of Bethesda. There people who were blind, crippled, or ailing lay waiting day after day, for it was said that an angel sometimes came to stir the waters and that the first person to enter the pool at such a time would be cured. When Jesus came up to

Jerusalem, he stopped one day at Bethesda, and there he found a man who had been waiting for a very long time. He had been ill for all of thirty-eight years. "I have no one to lift me into the waters when they are troubled," the man explained to Jesus. "This is why I cannot get well."

"Do you want to be well?" Jesus asked him. The man, in great surprise, answered that he did.

*"Then, stand up and walk!"* said Jesus. And the man rose to his feet immediately, and he was healed.

Now, Jesus went quietly away after this, but the Jewish leaders heard about it. Because it had been done on the sabbath, they were outraged. They found Jesus and questioned him. "My Father works on the sabbath, and so do I!" he told them. Now they were even more furious. Jesus of Nazareth was saying that he was equal to God! Throughout Jerusalem the people in power spoke cruelly of him, and planned how he might be killed.

# Food for the Hungry

While plots formed against him, Jesus left Jerusalem and walked once more upon the dusty roads of Galilee, preaching and bringing the good news of God's kingdom. With him and the disciples now came a number of women who loved Jesus and helped to look after him. Mary Magdalene was one of these; she had been possessed by seven demons until Jesus had healed her. There was also Joanna, the wife of Herod's steward, and a woman called Susanna, as well as several others who followed his teachings with great devotion and provided for his daily needs with their own funds.

And some Pharisees from Jerusalem followed Jesus now from place to place, closely watching everything he did. These men's hearts had hardened as their minds had been given over to the rules of religion, rather than the love of God; and they were greatly disturbed by the way Jesus behaved. They watched him as he told people to love and forgive one another before offering sacrifices to God. They watched him as he touched lepers to heal them; and they watched him as he sat down with great crowds all around him, seeking a moment's leisure for his midday meal.

"Look at that!" they said to one another. "He did not stop before eating to rinse his hands with the water of purification, as the Law prescribes! What a disobedient, dirty man this is!"

Jesus looked wearily up at them. "When will you learn," he

asked, "that it is not what goes into a person's mouth that makes him dirty; it is what comes out of it. Hear what I mean by that, if you have ears!"

"What did you mean?" the disciples asked him, after they had finished eating. "The Pharisees are very angry with you!" Jesus replied, "Let them be angry! They do not rule rightly; they are the blind leading the blind. It is not earth's dirt, it is human lies and cruel speech that makes people impure. From the dirty heart come words that do injury.

"Now come away with me," he said to them. "There is no rest for us here. We need to go for a time to a quiet place, where we may be refreshed." So the disciples went with him then in a boat across the lake, toward a lonely meadow on the other side. But the people saw this, and from all the towns and villages in that region they ran after the boat, along the shore. By the time Jesus approached the land, a tremendous throng of men, women, and children already awaited him. The grass of the meadow had been trampled under their feet, and the surrounding hills were echoing with their eager cries.

Love and pity filled the heart of Jesus as he saw them waiting there. He stepped ashore and, weary as he was, began again teaching them. The hours went by, and then it was night, and then another day. Still they did not leave, and after three days in that place, Jesus became concerned for them all, seeing that no one had had anything to eat.

At this time the disciples came to him and said, "Master, you should tell these people to go away now and buy themselves some food at the nearest village!" But Jesus replied, "No! They

are hungry; you feed them." The disciples were dismayed. "What, all of this crowd?" they exclaimed. "Who on earth has money enough for that?" And Jesus answered, "Go and see how many loaves of bread you have." So the disciples looked at their supplies and reported back to him, "We have five loaves left, and two fish."

"Very well," said Jesus. He commanded the crowd to sit down together in groups. Taking the loaves and the fishes in his hands, he looked to heaven and blessed them; then he divided them up and gave them to the disciples to set before the people.

Everyone there was very hungry, and gratefully they began to eat. They ate and they ate; yet there was always plenty more, and so they continued to eat until every single person was satisfied. When they had finished at last, twelve baskets were filled by the disciples with the scraps that remained.

Now, like a great wind, a murmur of excitement swept through the crowd, and then the murmur became a shout of triumph and joy. "It is a sign!" they cried. "This is the leader who will defeat our enemies! This is the warrior who will save Israel! He shall be our king!" And they rose up in a mass, trying to lay hands upon Jesus so that they could crown him king.

But Jesus slipped away from them and climbed swiftly far up into the hills. There as the night descended he stayed alone, and as the stars shone down on Galilee, Jesus remained there silently upon his knees, hour after hour, deep in prayer.

# A Different Kind of King

**W**hen he had come down from the hills, Jesus went again to the little town of Capernaum, where his ministry had begun. Many of his followers were disappointed in him now, because he would not let them crown him king. He stood before them in the synagogue at Capernaum, trying once more to make himself understood.

"You are here today," he told the people, "not because you know who I am but because you filled your bellies with the food I gave you. But what I bring you is so much more than that! God the Father has set his seal upon me. I have come to bring you not only food for your bodies but food for your souls, so that you may have eternal life."

And then Jesus said to them, "I am the bread of life. He who comes to me shall not hunger; and he who believes in me shall never thirst. Look! I am your nourishment! I have come down from heaven not to do my will but to do the will of him who sent me. I am giving myself to you so that you may live. Devour my teachings! Feed upon my words! Eat and drink my very being, and you will never die."

But at this, more people left him, saying, "What is this madman talking about? Is he not the son of Joseph, whose mother and father we know? Why does he say that he came down from heaven? How can we feed upon him?" And when Jesus saw them leaving, he turned to his twelve disciples and asked them, "Will you go away too?"

Simon Peter answered him, "Lord, where should we go? We know you. We have heard your words, and we believe." So they left that place together, crossed over the river Jordan, and began traveling north. Jesus knew of the death of John the Baptist and of the plots against his own life, but he also knew that his time had not come. He had to leave Galilee in order to complete his ministry.

As they walked along the road toward a town in the northern region called Caesarea Philippi, Jesus said to his disciples, "Who do people say now that I am?" They answered, "Some say, John the Baptist back from the dead, and others say, Elijah, or one of the other prophets." And then he asked them, "Who do you say I am?" And Peter replied, "You are the Christ, the Son of the living God!"

"Blessed are you, Simon Peter!" Jesus said. "No human being has taught you this; it was my Father, who is in heaven. You understand that mine is a heavenly kingdom, and I shall give you the keys to it. You are the rock on which I shall build my church!"

At this time, Jesus began to prepare his disciples for the future; and he explained to them that he must go someday soon to Jerusalem, and be crucified. When Peter heard it, he was overcome with anger and grief. He threw his arms around Jesus and cried, "No! God forbid that such a thing should ever happen to you!" But Jesus turned fiercely away from him and exclaimed, "Get behind me, Satan! Do not stand in my way! If you cannot accept this, then you take sides with human beings, against God!"

And he explained to his disciples that he must face trial for all that he was doing on earth, and be punished by death for it; and that, on the third day, he would rise again. Still the disciples did not understand.

Then, after they had been in the north for six days, Jesus took Peter, and John and his brother James, up on a high mountain with him to a place far from any town. There the sun shone brightly down upon the snow, and in the pure, high air all things glittered and blazed about them. But far beyond any brilliance the disciples had ever experienced was the figure of Jesus as they suddenly saw him standing there before them. The master they had followed for so long, the leader they had known and loved so well, was now transformed into a being of pure light, with his face and garments shining like the sun. As the amazed disciples continued to look up at him, they saw that Moses and Elijah had appeared beside Jesus and that the three were talking together.

Peter, as usual, was the first to speak his mind. "Lord," he blurted out to Jesus, "how good it is that we are with you now! If you wish, I will make three shelters, one for you, one for Moses, and one for Elijah." Peter was still speaking when a blazing cloud surrounded them all, and a voice from the cloud said, "This is my beloved Son, in whom I am well pleased! Listen to him!"

When the disciples heard this, they were filled with terror, and they fell to the ground, worshiping. But Jesus came and touched them, saying, "Rise up, and do not be afraid." And when they lifted up their eyes again, they saw only the sun shining on the snow, and Jesus standing there. As they came down the mountain together, Jesus commanded them, "Do not tell anyone of this vision until I have risen from the dead!"

Thus it was that the disciples began to understand that the kingship of Jesus was not one of worldly power, which passes away, but a thing of the spirit that is everlasting. When he began preaching to the people again, they heard him say, "I am the light of the world," and now the disciples knew that they had seen that light with their own eyes.

Gently and carefully, Jesus worked from now on to make his disciples ready for the time when he must leave them. He gave them power to forgive people's sins and to approach God directly on behalf of others' needs, just as he did himself. "Where two or three are gathered together in my name," he promised them, "there I will always be also."

So began the latter part of Christ's ministry, far from the crowds and throngs of Galilee, among strangers who heard his words with fresh astonishment, and often with grave doubt. "You must be possessed by a demon!" some said to him. "You dishonor my Father when you say that," Jesus replied. "He has sent me not for my own glory but to do his work so that you may glorify him. Truly I tell you, that if you abide by my teachings, you will have everlasting life. Your own ancestor Abraham rejoiced when he heard that I was coming to save you!"

"Abraham died hundreds of years ago!" cried the people. "You must be mad, to say that you have seen him!" And Jesus replied, "Before Abraham was, *I am.*"

# Faith That Moves Mountains

Now Jesus sent his disciples out into the countryside to preach and to heal as he had taught them. But, soon afterward, a man came to Jesus, crying, "Master, I beg you to help my son if you can, for your disciples have not been able to cure him!" And indeed, the man's son fell down in a terrible convulsion in front of Jesus, rolling about in agony and frothing at the mouth.

"O, how longer must I bear this?" Jesus exclaimed. "How much longer must I stay in this faithless, miserable world?" Then, to the boy's father, he said, "*If I can?* Of course I can help him, if only you believe it." And the man answered him in tears, "I believe, but, O Lord, help my unbelief!"

Jesus laid his hands upon the boy. "Depart from him, you evil spirit and never come back again!" he commanded. And the boy lay still as a corpse, but he was not dead; the demon had left him. Jesus helped him to rise, entirely well.

"Why could we not do it?" the disciples asked. "We tried our best." Jesus answered, "There are some evil spirits in this world that can only be conquered after much prayer. But I tell you truly that if you only had faith enough, you could command a mountain to be moved and it would move itself into the sea."

# Children of God

Jesus sat alone one day, thinking about his disciples. There were times when they seemed quite ready to do the work of the Father; but then again, they would behave as if they had forgotten everything he had taught them, or as if they had never understood him at all.

For example, Jesus knew that the disciples had been troubling themselves lately with an argument about which one of them was the greatest and the most important. He sighed. When would they learn the foolishness of such a question?

And now he saw that the village people were coming toward him, bringing their babies and little children to receive his blessing, as many families had done of late; and he saw his disciples going to meet them and turning them away. Perhaps they thought he did not want to be disturbed just now; perhaps they thought he did not want to be bothered with children at all.

Jesus stood up. "Let the children come to me!" he cried. Impatiently, he strode into the crowd. In their midst, he stooped down to put his arms around one of the littlest of the children, speaking gently to him. Then he lifted up the child in his arms and said to his disciples and all the people listening, "Truly I tell you, unless you welcome little ones such as this, you will never get into the kingdom of heaven! You must be gentle with all who are weak and helpless in this world; and never forget that the person who greets any child in my name, greets me." He smiled at the boy in his arms, and the child laughed joyously back at Jesus, reaching out a trusting little hand to touch his face.

"When you are able to look at the world as this child does," Jesus said, "then you will see God."

"O Master," cried the child's mother, "let me take him now so that he will not be any trouble to you. I only sought your blessing, for I want him to be a great and important man someday!"

Jesus did not answer her. Instead, he sat down, holding the little boy on his lap, and gathered all the other children close to him too, touching them tenderly and giving his blessing to them all. "These little ones are great and important to God already," he said, looking straight at his disciples. "No one on earth matters more to God than the least of these!" The disciples saw that he knew about their foolish arguments, and their faces burned with shame.

"Each one of these has a guardian angel in heaven," Jesus said, with his arms around the children, "and it is upon their angels that my Father's face continually shines. He will not stand for it if even one of them is lost. So, you parents and you older people, look upon them and beware! Betray their trust and I promise you, you will suffer for it. Truly I tell you, whoever leads a child into sin, it would be better for him if he had a heavy weight tied around his neck, and then he were cast into the sea."

# The Good Samaritan

Aproud man came to Jesus one day and said, "Master, I have heard that you teach us always to show kindness to our neighbors, but let me ask you this: Who is my neighbor? The world, after all, is filled with a great many ignorant and wicked people. Foreigners do not abide by our Law. The ways of strangers are different from mine, and I have no guarantee that they would show me kindness. Therefore, is my neighbor the man who lives in my own street, or is it some barbarian I do not know? And where will you draw the dividing line?"

"Once upon a time," Jesus replied, "there was a man going down from Jerusalem to Jericho. And he was attacked by thieves, who stripped him, and beat him, and ran away leaving him half dead. Now it happened that a priest of our Temple was traveling down that same road, and he saw the man lying there covered with blood; but he turned his face and crossed over the road, passing him by.

"And then came a Levite, one of the highest orders, who preaches the Law constantly to the people. And yet when he came to that place and saw the man dying, he did not stop. He, too, crossed over the road and went by on the other side.

"Next came a Samaritan, one of those barbarians you are talking about. And when the Samaritan saw the man lying there helpless, he had mercy on him. He went to the man and tenderly bound up his wounds, pouring on precious oil and wine to heal

them. Then he lifted the man up and put him on his own donkey and brought him to a nearby inn. He stayed overnight at the inn with the man, looking after him. The next morning he gave some of his own money to the innkeeper and told him, 'Take care of this man, and if more money than this is needed, I will pay it to you when I come back.' Now," continued Jesus, "let me ask you this: Which of the three, do you think, was fit to be called the neighbor of the man who fell among thieves?"

The proud man answered, "The one who showed mercy on him."

And Jesus said, "Yes. Now, you go and do the same."

Then Jesus said to the people, "Truly I tell you that on the Day of Judgment the Son of Man will come in all his glory, and he will separate the people on earth as a shepherd separates his sheep from his goats. There you will see God's dividing line! For those who are sent to his left hand will go to everlasting damnation. But he will say to those who are on his right, 'Come, you who are blessed by my Father, inherit the kingdom which was made ready for you at the world's beginning. For when I was hungry, you fed me; and when I was thirsty, you gave me something to drink. I was a stranger and you took me in; I was naked and you clothed me. I was sick and you cared for me; I was in prison and you came to visit me.'

"And then those who have done what is right will answer, 'Lord, we never saw you sick, or hungry, or suffering, or in prison. When did we ever do any of these things for you?'

"And the King of Heaven will say to them, 'Inasmuch as you have done this to the least human being on earth, you have done it to me.' "

# Eye of the Needle

Once again, Jesus began walking on the long road south. Messengers ran ahead of him, but he was not welcomed in every town, and this made the disciples angry. But Jesus only said, "Foxes have holes, and birds of the air have nests; but the Son of Man has no place to lay his head." And he continued on his way.

When he had come to a certain Judean town, a rich young man ran out to greet him and kneeled down at his feet. "Good teacher!" he cried eagerly, with his eyes sparkling, "what must I do to enter the kingdom of heaven, and have eternal life?"

Jesus smiled. "Why do you call me good?" he asked. "Only God is good, and you know his commandments already; they have been given to you by the Prophets and the Law."

At this, the young man's face shone with pride and delight. "I have obeyed every one of the commandments since I was a small boy!" he exclaimed. Jesus looked at him with love, and yet also with a measure of sadness. For the youth was dressed in a fine robe and he wore jeweled rings upon his fingers; yet in this very town there were many who had not enough to eat, and the young man must have known it. "One thing is lacking," Jesus told him. "Go and sell what you have and give it to the poor; then come and follow me!"

The young man grew pale, and rose to his feet. He stood for

a moment, staring at Jesus in dismay. Indeed, he was very, very rich, and his possessions were important to him. With tears in his eyes, he turned and went away.

And Jesus looked around and said sorrowfully to his disciples, "How hard it is for those who have money to enter the kingdom! I tell you, it is easier for a camel to go through the eye of a needle than it is for a rich man to find God."

Then Peter said to him, "But oh, what will become of us, Lord? For we have given up everything, and followed you." And Jesus replied, "Truly, those who give up what is dear in this world for my sake will receive a hundred times more in the age to come: brothers and sisters, mothers and children, houses and lands as well, and life everlasting!"

Jesus saw that there were many people around him who cared, like the rich young man, too much about material things, and he knew that their souls were in danger because of it. Therefore he told them this parable: "Once upon a time there was a rich man who dressed like a king and feasted in great splendor, day after day. At the door of his palace lay a beggar named Lazarus, filthy and covered from head to foot with open sores. Lazarus was so hungry that he yearned for the crumbs that fell from the rich man's table; and the dogs of the town gathered around him to lick his sores. One day he died, and angels carried him to rest in the arms of Abraham. Then the rich man died, and was buried; but he went straight to hell.

"Now the rich man looked up from his place of torment, and he saw Lazarus far, far away, resting with Abraham. And he called out, 'Father Abraham, have mercy on me! Send Lazarus only to dip his finger in cool water and touch my mouth with it, for I am in agony here in the flames!' But Abraham called to him, 'My child, you had your share of good things during your lifetime, while Lazarus was suffering. And because you did not help him then, there is now a great gulf between us, that no one can cross over.'

"Then the rich man said, 'I beg you, send Lazarus to my home and let him warn my five brothers, so that they may never come to this terrible place!' Abraham replied, 'Moses and the prophets have already warned them.' And Lazarus said, 'But, Father Abraham, they do not believe it! If someone comes back from the dead and tells them about it, then surely they will.' But

Abraham answered him, 'If they paid no attention to Moses and the prophets, then they will not believe my teachings even if someone should rise up from the dead.'"

Now, at this time Jesus was traveling in Galilee, and some friendly Pharisees came to him and said, "You had better leave this place quickly! Herod knows where you are, and he is going to kill you!" But Jesus said, "Go and tell that fox I shall continue with my work until I am finished with it. Today and tomorrow I heal, and I cast out demons; it is only upon the third day that my time will come. Yet in the meantime I shall go to the Holy City; for it is not right that a prophet should die anywhere but Jerusalem."

# Mary and Martha

Quite near to Jerusalem, in the town of Bethany, there lived a woman named Martha; and she had a sister named Mary and a brother named Lazarus. When Jesus came to Bethany, Martha welcomed him and brought him to stay in her house. Then she immediately began rushing around in a dither, making a tremendous fuss over all the arrangements she felt were proper for a guest.

But her sister, Mary, behaved quite differently. She sat down quietly at Jesus' feet and listened with all her heart and soul to his teachings. People came and went all day, in and out of the little house, but nothing took her attention from him.

At last it was time for the evening meal, and by now Martha was extremely tired and cross. She banged her pots and pans upon the oven and sighed loudly, but no one paid her any notice. Finally she stormed into the room where Mary sat beside Jesus and said, "Lord, don't you care at all that my sister has left me to serve you all alone? Tell her to come out here and help me!"

But Jesus said to her gently, "O Martha, Martha! You are making yourself frantic over so many details! But there is very little that we really need in this world—perhaps, in the end, there is only one thing. Mary has made a better choice than you. Come, do not try to take it away from her!"

# The Prodigal Son

It was amazing to the enemies of Jesus that he dared, even now, to go about unprotected from town to town, showing his concern for everyone he met. What a strange leader this was! Where were his armies? His weapons? What powers had he? Jesus of Nazareth treated everyone alike: men, women, and children, the rich and the poor, the priests, the tax collectors, the prostitutes. If he showed any preference, it was in giving even more of his energy to people who were in trouble: the sick and the disgraced, the sinners everywhere, and those with despair in their hearts. "Come to me, all you who are weary and heavy-laden," they heard him say. "My yoke is easy, and my burden is light."

And they were scandalized one day to see him welcoming a woman of the town who was well known as a sinner; for a long time she knelt before him, weeping, and with her tears she washed his feet, and with her hair she wiped them. What would he say to this? "Her sins, which are many, are forgiven," Jesus said, "for she has loved much."

What Jesus saw was the pain of a people who had failed to obey God's Law, as it had been given to them by Moses and the prophets. Some were too proud to receive his message, but many others were simply too guilty and too frightened. They could not understand the good news of God's kingdom, because, by now, they were afraid of God. And so Jesus told them this story:

There was once a man who had two sons; and the younger one came to him and said, "Father, give me my share of your property now!" So the father gave him his share, and the boy went away to a distant country. There he lived in a wild and foolish way, and soon he had spent all the wealth he had been given.

Famine and hard times came upon that land, and at last there was nothing for the young man to do but go and work for a local farmer, feeding pigs. Indeed, he himself was so hungry that he would have been glad to eat the garbage he offered to the animals, but no one gave him anything. Then, one day, he remembered who he was and where he had come from. He said to himself, "Here I am starving, while my father's hired servants are given all they need. I will go back to him and tell him I am sorry. Perhaps he will hire me."

So the young man rose up and began the long journey home. But his father had been watching and waiting for him, and he saw him a long way off, coming down the road, barefoot and in rags. With outstretched arms he ran to meet his son, and kissed him.

The young man said, "Father, I have done wrong, and I am so ashamed. I have led an evil life, and I have wasted all of my inheritance. I am no longer worthy to be called your son; I only beg you to let me work for you, and let me be treated as one of your servants from now on."

But the father only held him closer and kissed him more

tenderly. Then he called to his servants, "Quickly! Bring my best robe and put it on my son, and put a ring on his finger and shoes on his feet. And kill the fatted calf, for we shall eat and make merry today. This is my son who was dead, and he is alive again! This is my son who was lost, and now he is found!"

It was done, and the celebration began. But the youth's elder brother was working out in the fields, and when he heard music and dancing, he wanted to know what was happening. The servants told him, and he was furious. He went back to the house but refused to go inside, and his father came out to meet him and plead with him. "Father, it isn't fair!" he cried. "I have worked for you all these years and have never been disobedient, while that prodigal brother of mine has gone out and committed every kind of sin. You never gave a special feast for me, but now that he has wasted his inheritance, you give him everything, and you kill the fatted calf for him!"

"My dear son," the father replied, "do not be jealous! You are here with me always, and all that I have is yours. But it is fitting that we should all feast and be glad today, for your brother was lost, and now is found; he was far, far away from us, and now at last he has come home."

When Jesus had finished this story, he looked at the wondering faces around him and said, "Some of you are shepherds. Which one of you, if you had a hundred sheep and one was lost, would not go out and search until you found the missing one? And when you found it, would you not carry it tenderly home, and call in your friends and neighbors to rejoice with you?"

And then he said to them, "Fear not, little flock! It is your heavenly Father's good pleasure to give you his kingdom. And truly I tell you, whenever so much as a single sinner among you repents, there is rejoicing among all the angels."

# The Man

ow Jesus went quietly into Jerusalem for the feast of Tabernacles; and when he was coming out of the Temple on the sabbath, there was a man, who had been born blind, begging for alms. Jesus took pity on him; and he spoke to him, and touched his eyes with clay, and the man was healed. But the Pharisees heard of it, and in a great fury they hauled the man up before them and questioned him until he had told them the entire story.

But the Pharisees refused to believe that the man had really been blind since birth, and so they called in his parents and questioned them. The old people were frightened; they knew they

# Born Blind

would be punished if they said that Jesus was the Christ. And so they replied, "Yes, that is our son, and indeed he was born blind. We do not know how he has been cured. He is of age; ask him."

So the Pharisees called the man in again and told him, "Praise God for your eyesight, but do not praise this wicked Jesus. God would not have allowed him to heal you upon the sabbath! Now tell us what *really* happened."

"What is your problem?" the man replied. "What really happened was that *I was blind and now I can see*. Why do you want to hear the part about Jesus all over again? Do you want to become his disciples too?"

# Mercy and the Law

Early one morning, Jesus was sitting in the Temple teaching the people; and the scribes and the Pharisees decided that this would be a good time to set a trap for him. So they came to the Temple, bringing with them a woman who had been caught betraying her sacred marriage vows. According to the Law of Moses, she should now be stoned to death. Jesus could do nothing to help her—or so they thought—without breaking the Law himself.

Pale with terror and shame, the woman stood trembling before the crowd. "Teacher, you know the commandments. What shall we do with her?" the Temple officials asked. But Jesus only leaned down and began writing something with his finger in the dust. Again they asked, with triumphant smiles upon their faces, "Well, sir, what do you say?" And Jesus answered quietly, "Whichever one of you has never sinned, let him cast the first stone at her." Then he bent over once more and continued writing in the dust.

For a long moment no one stirred. Then, beginning with the eldest, the woman's accusers turned one by one and went away without saying another word. "Where have they gone?" Jesus asked the woman when they were alone. "Has no one stayed to condemn you?"

"No one, Lord," she replied, in tears. And Jesus said, "Neither do I condemn you. Go, and do not sin any more."

# Lazarus Raised

Once more, Jesus went quietly away to a place beyond the Jordan; and while he was there, he received a message that his good friend Lazarus, the brother of Mary and Martha, whom he loved, was mortally ill. Yet for a time Jesus did not stir; and he said to his disciples, "This illness will not end in death. It will end in glory to God, and in the Son's glorification." And after two more days he said to them, "Now let us go to Judea."

"You will surely be killed this time!" they protested. "Do not go!" But Jesus replied, "Our friend Lazarus is resting. I am going to awaken him." Then, seeing that they did not understand him, he said to them plainly, "Lazarus is dead. And for your sakes, I am glad that I was not there. What you see now will make you believe."

So they went together to Bethany, in Judea, and when they arrived, they found that Lazarus had already been in his tomb for four days. Friends and relatives had gathered to console Mary and Martha; but when Martha heard that Jesus was nearby she went running out to meet him, bitterly weeping. "O Master, if you had been here, my brother would not have died," she said. "Your brother will rise again," Jesus told her. And she said, "I know he will, at the time of resurrection, when the world comes to an end."

But Jesus said, "I am the resurrection. I am life. Whoever believes in me will have life after death. *Do you believe?*"

"O Master," she cried, "I believe you are the Son of God,

and whatever you ask of him, he will surely give you!" Then she ran into the house and whispered to Mary, "He is here!" Mary rose and went quickly to Jesus, and all the visitors followed her, thinking she meant to go and mourn at the tomb. But Mary went straight to Jesus and threw herself at his feet, crying, "Lord, if only you had been here, this would not have happened!"

Jesus gave a deep sigh. "See how he loved Lazarus!" the people told one another; for they were not able to understand the mighty forces that were stirring within him now. "Where have you put him?" Jesus asked, in a tone of great distress; and the people replied, "Lord, come and see." Jesus wept.

And when they came to the tomb, he commanded them to roll away the stone from it. Martha protested, "It is the fourth day! There will surely be a foul smell." But Jesus exclaimed, "Have I not told you that if you believe, you will see God's glory?" and so they rolled away the stone. "Thank you for hearing me, Father," Jesus said. "I know that you always hear me, but for the sake of these people I thank you. Now at last they will believe that you sent me." Then, in a loud voice, he cried, "Lazarus, come forth!" And as soon as he had spoken, the dead man rose and came walking out of his tomb alive, wrapped in all his gravecloths. Jesus said, "Unbind him. Set him free!" And so they did, and Lazarus lived again.

When word of this great miracle reached Jerusalem, the priests and elders were frightened, for they knew that their Roman overlords might make the entire nation suffer for deeds such as this. "We must get rid of this man Jesus somehow," they said.

# Day of Joy

Now Jesus turned his face toward Jerusalem, and he said to his disciples, "Go to the village and bring me the young donkey you will find tethered there. Tell anyone who asks you that the Master needs it but it will be returned." So they went into the village and found the

donkey, as he had said, and brought it to him. But it was only later that they remembered the words of the prophet Zechariah:

> *Rejoice and be glad, daughter of Zion!*
> *Behold, your king is coming to you,*
> *And he rides in peace upon a lowly beast.*

So it was that Jesus rode, on that day of joy, toward the Holy City with crowds of people rushing ahead to spread their garments in the dust and flinging down green palm branches for his humble mount to tread on. The people of Jerusalem had heard that Lazarus was raised, and they came running out to meet Jesus, cheering and shouting praises, until everyone was singing together:

> *Hosanna for the coming of David's kingdom!*
> *Blessed is he who comes in the name of the Lord,*
> *Hosanna in the highest!*

"You see, there is nothing we can do," the priests and the Pharisees said to one another. "Everyone in the world is running after him now." And they told Jesus, "Stop your people from making all this uproar!" But he replied, "Truly, I tell you that if the people were silent today, the stones on the ground would cry out."

# Jerusalem, Jerusalem

Jesus looked out over the splendid city that lay before him, so richly glowing with all the colors of earth and sky; and he heard the glad cries of the people, and the little children calling out to him, "Hosanna!" And again he wept, saying, "O Jerusalem, Jerusalem, how I have wanted to protect you! I would have gathered you in as tenderly as a hen shelters her brood beneath her wings. But you would not hear me calling; you would not come to me. You kill your prophets, and your enemies overtake you. Soon you will be utterly destroyed, for even now, you will not learn the things that make for peace!"

Despite the welcome he had received, Jesus knew that the time of his death was very near. The Roman rulers would crush any sign of real power among the Jews; and the Jewish officials wanted to be rid of him too, for Jesus rebuked and challenged them at every turn. Caiaphas, who was high priest that year, had already said to the Jewish council, "Let him be destroyed. It makes good sense that one man should die to save the rest of us."

It was near the time of the Passover feast. At dawn each day, people thronged to the Temple to hear Jesus teach; and day after day the Jewish leaders tested him with questions, seeking an excuse to have him arrested and put to death.

First the Pharisees came to him and said, "We know you

teach people to obey the laws of God, rather than of men. So tell us this: Should we Jews pay taxes to the Romans, or not?" And Jesus, seeing how they meant to trap him, answered, "Oh, you hypocrites! Show me the money for the tax." So they brought him a coin, and he asked them, "Whose image and whose name is on this coin?" And they said, "Caesar's." And Jesus told them, "Give it to Caesar, then. And give to God what is his." They went away, marveling at him.

Then the Sadducees came, and because they did not believe in life after death, they asked him this question: "Suppose a woman is widowed and then she marries again; and suppose this happens seven times, until she has had seven husbands in all. At the resurrection you speak of, whose wife will she be then?"

And Jesus answered them, "What fools you are! You do not know the power of God, and you do not know the Scriptures, either. It is written that God told Moses, 'I am the God of Abraham, and of Isaac, and of Jacob.' That should have told you that your ancestors still had life. As for the resurrection, marriage has no place in it; people live after death the way the angels in heaven do." When the crowd heard this, they were astonished at his teachings.

Hearing all the dispute, a scribe who liked the way he spoke came to Jesus and said, "Teacher, tell us which is the greatest of all the commandments." And Jesus said, "Hear, O Israel, the Lord our God is one God; and you shall love the Lord your God with all your heart, and with all your soul, and with all your mind, and with all your strength. This is the first commandment, and the second cannot be separated from it: You shall love your neighbor as yourself." The scribe, deeply moved, said to Jesus, "Sir, you speak the truth! And compared to this, our burnt offerings are unimportant."

"If you understand that," Jesus said, "you are very near to the kingdom of heaven. But woe to those who do not understand

it!" Then he turned to the crowd and said, "Woe to the hypocrites! Beware of your wicked leaders who care for appearances, not for faith or mercy or the Law! Woe to the Pharisees: Like whitewashed tombs, they make themselves look clean, but there is death and there is rottenness inside!"

Then he said to his disciples, "Truly I tell you, you are all brothers. And you have one Father, who is in heaven; and you have one Master, who is Christ." And after this, he taught them, in many parables, how they should serve God as good stewards of his riches and good caretakers of his estate. Like the maiden who waits for her bridegroom, he told them, his followers should keep the lamps of their souls forever trimmed, and brightly lit. And he taught them that the kingdom of heaven was like a great wedding feast, to which God would call them to be his honored guests. They must be ready for this at any time, he said, for no one knew when that day would come.

And on the last day when Jesus taught them, he cried out to them, saying, "Whoever sees me sees the Father, who sent me! Whoever hears my teachings and does not follow them, I do not judge him; for I did not come to judge, but to save the world. Yet he will be judged, by the word that I have spoken, for my word has come from God."

As they left the Temple that evening, the disciples looked up at its vast arches and its shining ornaments; and they said to Jesus, "What a magnificent building it is!" But he replied, "The time will come when every stone of it has been torn down. And heaven and earth will someday pass away; but my word will never die."

# The Last Supper

ow Jesus had withdrawn once more to Bethany; but the day came when the Passover lamb must be sacrificed, and he told Peter and John to make arrangements for the feast. "Where shall it be?" they asked. "Go into Jerusalem," he told them. "A man carrying a jar of water will meet you there, and you must follow him into the house where he will go. Tell the owner of that house, 'The Master wishes to celebrate the Passover here with his disciples,' and he will show you a large upper room." So the disciples obeyed him, and it all came about just as he had said.

When it was evening, Jesus came to the house, and to the upper room. There he sat at the table with the twelve disciples. "I have greatly desired to share this meal with you before my suffering," he said. "After this, I shall not eat again, or drink of the fruit of the vine, until God's purpose is fulfilled." Then he took bread, and when he had given thanks, he broke it and gave it to his disciples, saying, "Take, eat. This is my body which is broken for you. In days to come, do this in remembrance of me." And then he took a cup, and when he had given thanks, he gave it to them, saying, "Drink of it, all of you, for this is my blood of the New Covenant, which is poured out for you and for many, for the forgiveness of sins. Do this, as often as you drink it, in remembrance of me."

And as they began their feast, Jesus said, "One who is now sharing this meal will betray me."

"Who is it, Lord?" the disciples asked, in great alarm. "His hand is upon the table now," Jesus replied. "He has dipped his bread into the same dish with me." Sorrowfully, the disciples

began discussing the matter, but soon their talk had turned into a dispute about which of them was the most important.

When Jesus heard this, he rose from the table and, putting aside his outer garment, he wrapped a towel around his waist and poured some water into a bowl. Then, like the lowliest of all household slaves, he began to wash the feet of his disciples and dry them upon the towel he wore. Seeing this, Simon Peter cried, "Lord, you shall never wash my feet!" But Jesus answered him, "If I do not wash you, then you have no part in me." And Peter said quickly, "Lord, not only my feet, but my head and my hands as well!"

After he had finished and put on his robe again, Jesus said to them, "Do you know what I have done? I have set an example for you. If I, who am your Master, have done this thing, then you must treat others in the very same way. He who would be greatest among you must be the servant and the slave of all."

Then he looked at the disciple who was called Judas Iscariot. He broke off a piece of bread and dipped it into his dish and offered it to Judas. "What you are going to do, do quickly," Jesus said to him. And as Judas Iscariot received this gift, Satan took full command of him. Already he had been stealing money from the disciples; now he meant to earn more by betraying Jesus to his enemies. He took the bread and went quickly from the house; and it was nighttime now.

To the disciples who remained, Jesus said, "My children, I am still with you for a little while. And now I give to you a new commandment: You must love one another as I have loved you. By this, all mankind will know that you are my disciples."

"Lord, where are you going?" Simon Peter asked.

"Where I am going now you cannot follow me," Jesus said. "Later, you will follow me." But Peter insisted, "Lord, let me come! I will follow you to prison and to death! I will lay down my life for you."

"Simon, Simon," said Jesus, "this very night, before the cock crows, you will deny three times that you have ever known me. Satan asked to have you so that he might sift you down like grain. But I have prayed that your faith will not fail you; and so, one day, you must bring that faith to your brothers and strengthen them."

"Do not leave us, Lord," the disciples begged.

"Do not let your hearts be troubled," Jesus answered. "Believe in God, and believe in me. In my Father's house there are many rooms, and I go to prepare a place for you. When I come again, I will gather you up so that you may be close to me. And you do know where I am going." Philip said, "Lord, please show us the Father, so we may see what he looks like. We don't know where you are going; we don't know the way."

"I am the way, and the truth, and the life," said Jesus. "In me you have heard the Father's word, and you have seen his works. I am the true vine, and my Father is the grower. I am the vine, and you are the branches that must bear fruit. You did not choose me, I chose you; and not as my slaves, but as my friends. *I will not leave you desolate.* In a little while, you will not see me for a time. Then again, in a little while, you will see me."

"What do you mean, 'in a little while'?" the disciples asked, becoming more and more alarmed.

"When a woman gives birth, she suffers pain," Jesus replied, "but soon she forgets it, in her joy that a human being has been brought into the world. So you will suffer now, for I must be lifted up from the earth in order to draw all people to me." And in saying this, he again foretold the manner of his death.

"For my sake you will be hated as I have been," he warned them. "The time will come when people will believe anyone who kills you is doing a service to God. Still, you must not be afraid. I came from the Father and now I go back to him. This will help you, for if I did not go, the Comforter could not be sent to you. But I will send the Comforter, who is the spirit of Truth, and he will guide you. Until now you have asked for nothing in my name. After this, if you pray to the Father for anything, he will give it to you for my sake. Ask and you will receive; and your joy will be complete."

"And now I leave you peace," Jesus said to them. "I give you my peace, which is not of the world. And although you must suffer, yet be of good cheer, for I have conquered the world."

And when he had said these things, Jesus lifted up his eyes to heaven and said, "Father, the hour has come. Glorify your Son, so that your Son may glorify you. Holy Father, I ask you to guard my disciples, as I have done. Give them your Truth; hold them forever close. Love them that they may be one, as we are one. Righteous Father, the world has not known you. But these few did believe that you sent me; help them, and help all those who will believe it, in times to come. Let them share in the love you have had for me, since long before the world began." Then he said to the disciples, "Come, rise up and let us go from here."

# The Garden
# of Gethsemane

Then Jesus went with his disciples to a garden on the Mount of Olives, a place called Gethsemane, where he had often withdrawn in private before. Directing them to wait for him, he went on into the garden, sighing now and deeply shaken with distress; and he brought with him Peter, and John and James the sons of Zebedee. "My soul is grieved to the point of death," he told them. "Stay here, and watch with me." Then a little farther into the darkness he went, and he fell upon the ground and prayed, "Abba, O my dear Father, if it can be, take this cup away. And yet, not my will but your will be done." And when he had poured out his heart, he turned to his disciples and saw that they had fallen fast asleep. "Could you not watch with me one hour?" he cried. "Pray for yourselves, that you may be saved from the time of trial! For indeed, the spirit is willing, but the flesh is weak."

Again Jesus began to call upon his Father, and now he was in such agony that his sweat was like great drops of blood falling upon the ground. In a little while he called again to the disciples, but their sorrow had tired them so, that again they had nodded off to sleep. Once more he chided them, and waked them, and went back to his prayers. And as Jesus was crying out for the third time to God in his anguish, Judas Iscariot was already drawing near. Up the Mount of Olives he was leading a group of armed guards and elders from the Temple, so that Jesus could be captured quietly in his place of retreat. They had been glad to learn where they might find him far from the common people who loved him, and they had paid Judas thirty pieces of silver for his help. "I will go straight to Jesus and kiss him upon the cheek," Judas told them. "By that you will know which one to seize."

For the third time, Jesus now rose from his prayers. When he found the disciples asleep again, he said, "Rise up now, and let us be going. The hour has come. My betrayer is at hand." And while he was still speaking, Judas entered the garden at the head of his band. He went to greet Jesus with a kiss, saying, "Hail, Master!"

"Why are you here, friend?" Jesus asked. "Will you betray the Son of Man with a kiss?" The guards laid their hands upon Jesus; and at this, Peter leapt forward and attacked them with a sword, striking the chief priest's servant and cutting off his ear. "No more of this!" said Jesus. "Those who take up the sword shall perish by the sword." And he touched the wounded man, and healed him.

Then he turned to the people of the Temple and said, "Why do you come for me with weapons, as if I were a criminal? Day after day I sat in the Temple, teaching, and you did not seize me. But all this has happened because the Law and the Prophets must be fulfilled. This is your hour, and such is the power of darkness."

So they took him away, to bring him up before the high priest, Caiaphas, and now he was surrounded by a mob of people who were carrying swords and clubs. Jesus had to go with them all alone, for as soon as the disciples understood the danger they were in, every one of them turned and fled into the night.

# Trial and Agony

By torchlight Jesus was brought now, bound like a common thief, into the stronghold of the high priest, Caiaphas. At a safe distance Peter followed; and he saw the guards tormenting Jesus and making a mockery of him. In the courtyard of the palace, trying to hide his face, Peter stopped beside a brazier to warm himself, and in the glow of its fire he was recognized by one of the palace servants. "This man was also with Jesus," she said. "What do you mean?" Peter said. "I do not know him." Someone else insisted, "You are one of his disciples!" but again Peter denied it. Then the bystanders said to him, "Surely you are one of them, for you are also a Galilean." And now, with a great oath, Peter exclaimed, "I do not know the man!" As he spoke, a cock crowed in the darkness, and Jesus turned toward Peter and looked at him. Then Peter remembered his prophecy, and burst into tears; and he left the courtyard, weeping bitterly.

Early the next morning, Jesus was taken before the Sanhedrin, the high court and council of the Jews. Alone and silent, he stood before the crowd as witnesses were brought forward to condemn him. "He said he would destroy our Temple!" one man said, and other tales were told against him; but nothing could be proved, nor did any two witnesses agree. "Have you no answer to these charges?" Caiaphas asked. But Jesus would say nothing at all. Finally the chief priest rose up and cried to him, "In the name of the living God I command you to tell us if you are the Christ, the Son of God!" And at this, Jesus answered him, "I am. And you will see the Son of Man sitting at the right hand of Power, coming with the clouds of heaven."

Caiaphas tore his garments and shouted, "What more do we need than this? He has spoken blasphemy! He deserves to die!" And they held a vote; and every one of the Sanhedrin condemned Jesus to death. The men who were holding Jesus struck him, and mocked him, and spat in his face. But when Judas Iscariot saw that he had been condemned, he told the priests, "This man is innocent, and I have sinned." He tried to give them back their thirty pieces of silver, but they only laughed at him; and so he threw the money down on the floor of the Temple and ran away and then he hanged himself.

Now the enemies of Jesus brought him before the Roman governor, whose name was Pilate. "This man is guilty of blasphemy, for he says he is Christ the King," they declared to Pilate. "He stirs up the nation, and leads the people astray; the penalty for this is death!" Pilate looked at Jesus, wondering what to do. He wished that the Jews would settle their own quarrels without bothering him. "Are you the King of the Jews?" he asked Jesus. "You have said it," Jesus replied, and then he would say no more. "Do you not know that I have the power to crucify you?" Pilate cried.

"The only power you have over me was given from above," Jesus answered calmly. "I have no soldiers to defend me now because my kingship is not of this world. I have come into the world to bear witness to the Truth."

"What is truth?" Pilate asked bitterly. Then he told the Temple officials, "Since he is a Galilean, this man's innocence or guilt is no concern of mine. Ask Herod what to do with him."

Herod, the governor of Galilee, was delighted when they brought the famous Jesus of Nazareth before him. How exciting it would be, he thought, to watch this Jew from the back country do a miracle or two! But Jesus only stood quietly looking at Herod and would not speak to him at all. The priests and courtiers stood by, loudly accusing him, and soon Herod grew bored. He and his guards dressed Jesus up in fine clothes to make fun of him, and sent him back to Pilate again.

An angry mob had gathered, meantime, outside Pilate's quarters, crying out for Jesus to be crucified. The unhappy governor saw that he must make a decision soon. "Have nothing to do with that innocent man," Pilate's wife told him, "for I have had a dream about him that terrifies me." Pilate remembered the custom in Jerusalem that, at the Passover every year, one prisoner could be freed; and so he went before the crowd and asked whether they would have him let Jesus go, or a prisoner called Barabbas, who was a robber and a rebel against Rome.

"Give us Barabbas!" cried the mob. "Then, what shall I do with Jesus, who has done no wrong?" he asked. "Crucify him!" was the reply. Again Pilate hesitated; but then he heard them say, "Jesus tells us not to give tribute to Caesar! You are no friend of Caesar's if you let him live!" Now Pilate was frightened, for his own position depended entirely upon Caesar's good will. He took a basin of water and washed his hands in it before the crowd.

"Look," he told them, "this is to show you that I take no responsibility for this man's death." Having said this, he gave the order for Barabbas to be freed and Jesus to be crucified.

So the soldiers led Jesus away to the death he had prophesied. But first, according to custom, he had to be scourged; and under this terrible torture with a heavy whip and flails of metal spikes, many a strong man had died. Jesus did not. Broken and bleeding, he rose to his feet; and they put a purple robe on him and thrust upon his head a crown of thorns, spitting on him and shouting amid their scornful laughter, "Hail, King of the Jews!"

Out to a place called Golgotha after this they made him walk, carrying his own cross; and when he stumbled, fainting, they seized a man named Simon of Cyrene, who was in the crowd, and made him carry it the rest of the way. At the place of execution, the weeping women who had followed after him came to Jesus offering wine mixed with myrrh to help his pain, but he would not take it; and then the soldiers stripped him, and nailed his hands and feet to the cross, and he was lifted up from the ground in agony. "Father, forgive them," he said, "they know not what they do."

This was at the third hour of the morning. "Save yourself now, if you are Christ!" the bystanders jeered. "Come down from the cross!" And on either side of Jesus, two despised criminals were also being crucified. One began to curse at him; but the other said, "Jesus, remember me when you come into your kingdom." And Jesus answered him, "Truly I tell you, this day you shall be with me in paradise."

Near the cross stood Mary the mother of Jesus, silently looking up at her firstborn son. With her stood John, the disciple Jesus loved, and Mary Magdalene. Jesus looked at his mother, and then at John. "Lady, this is your son," he said to his mother. To John he said, "Behold, your mother." And slowly the hours went by.

And at the sixth hour a great darkness covered the noonday sun. Jesus cried out, "My God, my God, why have you forsaken me?"

# Death and Resurrection

At the ninth hour, Jesus said, "I thirst." So the soldiers held up to his lips a sponge that was filled with vinegar; and when he had received it, Jesus said, "It is finished." Then in a loud voice he cried, "Father, into your hands I commit my spirit!" and having said this, he breathed his last. From the foot of the cross a Roman centurion gazed up at him in wonder and exclaimed, "Truly, this was the Son of God!"

The earth shook violently at the moment of his death, and the veil of the Temple was torn asunder. The people of Jerusalem were stricken with awe and fear. A secret follower of Jesus', named Joseph of Arimathea, got up his courage that evening and went before Pilate, asking to have the body of Jesus for burial. "What, is he dead already?" asked Pilate in surprise. His soldiers said yes: They had stabbed the body of Jesus with a spear, to make sure.

Mary the mother of Jesus was still standing there when Joseph came to take the nails from her son's body and to take him down from the cross. Carefully they wrapped the broken form in a shroud of linen and wrapped a napkin around its head. Then, with Mary Magdalene and a few other women from Galilee, they went sorrowing with their precious burden to a garden place nearby, where Joseph had a tomb. It was nighttime now, and the holy hours of the sabbath had begun. The day after

next, the body could be properly anointed. For the time being, they could only place it in the tomb, with a great stone rolled against the entrance so that it could not be moved. And after they had left, the high priests sent guards there to stand watch. They did not want any more trouble from the followers of Jesus of Nazareth.

Early on Sunday morning, Mary Magdalene went with two other women into the garden, bringing spices for the rites of burial. When she came to the tomb, she saw the great stone set aside; and she ran back to Peter and John, crying out in her terror, "They have taken our Lord away!" So Peter and John came running in the early light of the dawn all the way up from the city; and John ran faster, so that he was the first to reach the tomb. He looked in and saw only the empty shroud. Then he stopped, overcome with emotion, and could not bring himself to go inside. But Simon Peter raced up after him and plunged in, so that he was the first to see not only the shroud lying there but also the napkin, now rolled up and placed separately. The two men stared and stared; and then they looked at one another. Only Jesus himself would have done such a thing. He had been dead, and now he was alive again. They understood this; and yet their shock was so great that they went away without saying a word.

Mary Magdalene stood by the empty tomb, weeping and lamenting. "Lady, why do you weep?" she heard a voice say. She turned, and seeing a man she thought was the gardener, she cried out, "If you have taken him, sir, please tell me where he is!" But it was Jesus. And he spoke to her again, saying, *Mary*. Then she knew him, and she sank to her knees, kissing his feet. In

Hebrew she said, *Rabboni!* which means *Master.* Then he spoke to her again; yet, when she told all of this later to the disciples, they did not dare to believe it.

For by now, hidden away in the city, the remaining disciples had sunk into despair. Their Master had suffered the cruelest of deaths; he was gone from them, and his enemies would surely try to murder them, too. All the long day they grieved and mourned and trembled, barricading themselves behind locked doors, unable to think what the future might bring. Then, in the evening they suddenly looked up and found Jesus in the room with them, standing there in their midst. "Peace be with you," he said. For a moment, they were too stunned and terrified to answer him.

"Give me something to eat," he told them. "Look, I am not a ghost. It is I, myself. Come touch me! See, I am made of flesh." Eyes wide with wonder, the disciples gathered around him and touched him. Then the disciple named Thomas, who was filled with doubt, put his hand upon the wounds. "My Lord and my God!" he said, and fell to his knees. The disciples had nothing to offer Jesus but a little broiled fish, but they gave that to him, and he gave thanks, and ate it.

"O men of little faith!" he chided them. "I told you when I was with you that it had all been written, in the Law and the Prophets and the Psalms. My suffering was necessary for the world's salvation. It was prophesied that I would rise on the third day; and I have risen. You are my witnesses. Now, for a time, you must stay here in the city. But I am going to our Father, and then you will be clothed with power from on high.

"Beginning in Jerusalem, then," he told them, "you must go

forth and preach my word to every nation. You must baptize the people, and heal them; you must teach them repentance, and the forgiveness of sins. I have risen now, and truly I tell you, I will be with you always, to the end of time."

# Birthday of the Church

**J**esus had risen. Those who had feared to believe it at first were now convinced of the fact, for he had appeared to them more than once over a period of forty days, not only in Jerusalem but in villages nearby, and by the Sea of Galilee. Again he had broken bread with them as before, and they could see that he was no ghostly spirit. All in all, Jesus was seen by more than five hundred people in Israel before his visible form was withdrawn from the earth. And when it was time for him to go to the Father, his disciples saw him taken up into the same shining cloud of holiness that had been witnessed by prophets in ages past.

It was a small group of people, even so, who gathered in Jerusalem after this to pray together and to consider what their future might be. Peter was there, and James and John. Also Andrew, Philip and Thomas, Bartholomew and Matthew, James the son of Alphaeus, Simon and Jude. A man named Matthias was chosen to fill the place of Judas Iscariot; and Mary the mother of Jesus was with them, together with his brothers and several other women. The twelve disciples knew that they must now become apostles—messengers and witnesses, that is—bringing the news of their Lord's teachings, and of his resurrection, to all people; but it was a frightening time and place for them to begin. In obedience to his command, they waited quietly together in the city, praying that Jesus might soon send them the power and the comfort that

340

had been promised from on high. Without the help of the Holy Spirit, the little band of men and women knew that they could accomplish nothing at all.

Then came the day called Pentecost, when all devout Jews gave thanks to God for the early sheaves of their new-planted crops. And as the same group gathered together, they suddenly heard the sound of a great wind rushing and surging all around them; and they knew at once that this wind was the breath and the spirit of God. Then a light appeared that moved among them like tongues of flame, and the light descended to touch each one. At this moment, they all began to speak aloud in the tongues of other nations, preaching the glory of God.

An astonished crowd soon gathered to listen, and people asked one another, "How is it that they can speak the languages of Persia now, and of Egypt and of Rome, so that all the foreigners among us can understand them? Are these men not from Galilee?" And some people mocked them, saying, "They must be drunk! They have had too much new wine."

Now Peter stood up, with the other eleven, to address the crowd. "People of Jerusalem!" he cried, "Listen carefully to what I say! These men have not been drinking. What you see and hear is the outpouring of the Holy Spirit upon us. Do you not remember what was taught by the prophet Joel?

> *In days to come, says the Lord,*
> *I will pour out my spirit on all mankind.*
> *Your sons and daughters shall prophesy,*
> *Your young people shall see visions,*
> *And your old people shall dream dreams. . . .*

"This is what is happening, and the reason for it is that Jesus

Christ of Nazareth has fulfilled all of our ancient prophecies. He was dead, but God has raised him up again, and we are his witnesses. Jesus was the Messiah from the House of David who was promised to you again and again, all these long years. And now you can be certain that this same Jesus, whom you handed over to be crucified, God has made both Lord and Christ!"

The people who heard this were stricken to the heart, and they asked Peter and the other apostles, "What shall we do?" Peter told them, "You must repent. You must be baptized in the name of Jesus Christ for the forgiveness of your sins, and then you will receive the gift of the Holy Spirit from the Lord our God." For a long time Peter continued speaking to them; and such was the power of his persuasion that some three thousand people immediately joined the little band. Sharing freely everything they owned and breaking bread together as Jesus had commanded, they lived as one large family in Jerusalem, and every day they went to the Temple, praising God. When others saw how the followers of Jesus behaved, they very much admired them, and many more came to join them day by day.

Now, one afternoon as Peter and John were going to the Temple for prayers, it happened that a man who was badly crippled was being carried nearby on a litter. This man always begged for alms at a place called The Beautiful Gate, for he had been lame since his birth, and he could make a living in no other way. When he saw Peter and John, he asked them for money. But, to his surprise, they did not give him any. Instead, they told him, "Look at us!" and they looked straight into his eyes. Then Peter said, "I have no silver or gold, but I will give you what I do have. In the name of Jesus Christ, stand up and walk!" And the man went into the Temple, walking and jumping and leaping, and praising God.

Year after year, the people of Jerusalem had seen this man lying crippled at The Beautiful Gate. Now he was well, and word of it spread throughout the city. More and more people joined the apostles, and this infuriated the elders who had handed Jesus over for crucifixion. They called for Peter and warned him never to mention the name of Jesus again. And when he and the other apostles disobeyed this order, they were all arrested and thrown into jail.

But an angel of the Lord came to them by night as they lay in jail and opened the gates for them. "Go and stand in the Temple!" the angel told them. "Preach salvation to the people." So the apostles went to the Temple and began preaching there at dawn. Meanwhile the full Sanhedrin had assembled for a solemn trial, but when they sent for the apostles, they were told, "The gates were locked, the guard was on duty—but the men are gone! Even now they are preaching again in the Temple."

"Arrest them again, but beware of the people," said the elders. Again the apostles were brought before them and accused. Peter spoke for them: "Obedience to God comes before obedience to men," he said. "It was you who condemned Jesus, but we are eye witnesses that God has raised him from the dead." Many in the Sanhedrin wanted the apostles put to death on the spot for this, but a Pharisee named Gamaliel offered wiser counsel. "Wait and see," he said. "God will decide their fate in time." And so the apostles were spared for the present, and after being given a whipping, were released.

For the task of giving away food each day to the needy, seven good workers were now chosen by the community, and one of these was a man of great power and grace called Stephen. Before long, some people of Jerusalem who had been arguing with him decided to accuse Stephen before the Sanhedrin. "He speaks in the name of Jesus the Nazarene, against God and

against the Temple," these false witnesses swore. And the high priest asked Stephen, "Is this true?"

With a shining face Stephen replied. He recounted the nation's history from the time of Abraham and reminded the Sanhedrin that Moses himself had been rejected by the people. "You have done this again and again," he told them. "You were given the Law by angels, but you have not kept it. Now you have murdered Jesus Christ, just as you did away with every one of the prophets who foretold his coming!"

The audience was in an uproar by now; but in a blaze of holy passion Stephen stared upward and said, "I can see him now! A rift in heaven—and look! There is Jesus at God's right hand!"

"Blasphemy! Blasphemy!" shrieked his listeners, clapping their hands over their ears. Then a mob rushed to seize him, and they all dragged him away to be stoned to death. "Lord Jesus, receive my spirit," Stephen exclaimed as he sank to his knees under a hail of stones. And as he breathed his last, he prayed, "Forgive them, Lord."

# On the Road to Damascus

**A** man named Saul stood watching Stephen die. *Good,* he thought. *Every one of these wicked fools should be destroyed!* Saul was an educated man, a deeply devout Jew and a Pharisee; and by birth he was also a citizen of Rome. It is not surprising that he despised this strange, new group of men and women who challenged the authorities. He saw them upsetting the very order of the universe, all for the sake of a simple Galilean who had died in disgrace.

Thus in a righteous fury Saul set out to wipe the followers of Jesus from the face of the earth. In a short time he was known as their greatest persecutor, one who would hunt and punish them wherever they might be. It was for such a search of terror among the citizens of Damascus that Saul set out one day on a journey north, carrying papers that gave him power of seizure and arrest.

The distant spires and palms of the city were in view; the sun blazed down upon Saul and his two traveling companions; and then, suddenly, a greater light surrounded Saul, poured forth from a source far mightier than the sun. Within an instant its brilliance had utterly blinded him, and he fell helpless to the ground. Then he heard a voice saying, "Saul, Saul, why do you persecute me?" His companions stood by, astonished and trembling, for although they, too, could hear the voice, they could see no one.

"Lord, who are you?" cried Saul. And the voice answered, "I am Jesus, whom you are persecuting. Get up now and go into the city. Then you will be told what to do." So Saul rose and went into Damascus, but his friends had to lead him by the hand, for he was still blind. For three days afterward he took nothing to eat or drink but kept to himself in constant prayer.

Meantime one of the faithful, a man named Ananias, who lived in the city, was told in a vision by the Lord, "Go to Straight Street and ask at the house of Judas there for a man named Saul. He will be expecting you." Ananias replied, "Lord Jesus, this is a dangerous man! He has come here to arrest anyone who calls upon you." But Jesus said to him, "Even so, you must go. I have chosen this man to bring my name before the unbelievers of the world." And so Ananias went and found Saul and laid his hands upon him. "Brother Saul," he said, "I am sent by the Lord Jesus, who appeared to you, so that you may have your sight back and receive the Holy Spirit." Immediately, Saul felt as if a veil had dropped from his eyes, and he could see again. In Jesus' name he was then baptized, and he took some food and began to regain his strength.

In one enormous moment, the life of a man had been transformed; and the later history of Saul the Pharisee would be filled with events equally amazing and wonderful. At present, however, he was a man who needed to be alone for a time with his God, coming to know the nature of the loving power that had seized him. "I did not discuss it with any human being," he wrote years afterward to his Christian friends. "Instead, I withdrew immediately to Arabia." And indeed, it was three long years before Saul was heard from again.

# Sowing of the Seeds

During the persecutions after Stephen's death, many believers fled into the countryside, and this was one thing that helped the early church to grow. Wherever they went, the followers of Jesus brought with them the memory of his teachings and the news of his resurrection from the dead. Like the gospel seeds that had been sown in his parables, their words were sometimes received in such a way that they could take firm, deep root.

One of these travelers was Philip, who had been a disciple since the time when Jesus himself had been baptized. For a while, he taught in Samaria, gathering many new believers there. Then, one morning, he began walking from Jerusalem toward the town of Gaza. A vision had come to him, telling him that he should be on that stretch of desert road on a certain day at high noon. Now he had a sense that something extraordinary was about to happen; and he looked up and saw a chariot moving toward him on the road. "Go and meet that chariot!" the Holy Spirit told him, and Philip began to run.

Now, it happened that the man in the chariot was a high-ranking official from Ethiopia, one who was, in fact, treasurer to the queen. When Philip came closer, he could see a great, dark-skinned man in fine silks and jewels; and then he heard something very surprising indeed. The foreigner was reading aloud to himself from ancient Jewish Scriptures! As Philip arrived, the words that he heard were these:

*The Servant of God has not sinned,*
*He is innocent.*
*Like a lamb he is led to the slaughter;*
*He does not protest. . . .*

Here the Ethiopian stopped in puzzlement, and looked up at Philip. "I cannot understand this without some guidance," he remarked. "Tell me, is the prophet Isaiah speaking of himself here, or is the man who suffers someone else?"

"I can help you," said Philip, and the Ethiopian official invited him to ride in the chariot. Then, as they went along together, Philip explained it all to him: how Jesus of Nazareth had been the one foretold by Isaiah and the other prophets; how he had come from God into the world; how he had suffered and died to save us all, and then had been raised up again.

The Ethiopian was deeply moved. After a time he said, "Look, there is some water by the road. May I be baptized here and now? I believe with all my heart and soul that Jesus Christ was the Son of God!" Philip saw that the man meant what he said. So, together, they went to the water, and Philip baptized him in the name of Jesus Christ. And the Ethiopian went on his way, rejoicing.

Peter, meantime, was preaching and baptizing in the towns along the coast. One day he was in Jaffa; and he went up to the rooftop of the house where he was staying so that he could spend the hour before the midday meal in prayer. As he opened his heart to God, a strange and troubling vision came to him. He saw a great cloth let down from heaven, containing every sort of living creature, and a voice from heaven told him that they were all intended for his nourishment. "The Law of Moses forbids those that are unclean!" he cried. But God answered him, "You are wrong to say that, for I myself have made them all."

The next day, Peter was pacing about the house struggling with himself over the meaning of this vision when a knock came at the door. It was a messenger from a man named Cornelius, who wanted urgently to see him. Now, Cornelius was a kind and courteous man, but he was not a Jew; and suddenly Peter understood what he had been shown. He went to Cornelius immediately, and entered his house.

In great humility, Cornelius prostrated himself before Peter. "Come, come—get up! After all, I am only a man," said Peter. And then he spoke to Cornelius and his household, saying, "I have had a vision, and it has taught me something. The old Law said that Jews should not mingle with people of other nations, but I understand now that no one is unclean. God made us all, and he does not have any favorites. He has worked through the Children of Israel especially, but his Son, Jesus Christ, is Lord of everyone!"

When Cornelius and his family heard this they were overjoyed, and then, as Peter continued speaking to them about the life and teachings of Jesus, he suddenly saw them seized before his eyes by the Holy Spirit. They spoke in foreign tongues, all praising God; and before he left them, Peter baptized every one.

"We hear you have been visiting the uncircumcised, and eating with them!" said the members of the Jerusalem church when Peter returned to them, and they were much displeased. "How could I have refused the water of baptism to those people?" Peter asked. "It is true that they have always been pagans, but now they believe in our Lord, and what happened to them was very much like our own Pentecost." When his friends had heard the whole story, they were content. "Obviously," they said, "God wants to save even those who have not kept his ancient covenant."

There were many surprises like this during the time when the church was beginning, but nothing quite so astonishing as the news that now arrived from Damascus. A man had suddenly appeared there, preaching the word of Jesus Christ with such radiance and power that the entire city was in a tumult. New disciples gathered about him day by day, and the officials of the Jewish community were so outraged that there was talk already of having him put to death. The new teacher must have known this, but he went boldly on with his ministry.

Who was this man? He was Saul the Pharisee, who had

once been their bitterest persecutor and their most dangerous enemy. "What does this mean?" the people in Jerusalem asked. "Can he be serious? How could we ever begin to trust such a person?" And others said, "Nothing is impossible for God. Let us wait and see."

But Saul was serious, and his followers in Damascus understood the great danger he was in. Again and again they warned him, and finally they came to him one night telling him that he must flee. Watches had been posted by the authorities at every gate to arrest him, but they had a plan.

And so it was that the mighty Pharisee climbed into a basket, and by having it let down over the walls in the dead of night he made his escape. Alone and on foot he crept away in the dark, bringing with him a message that would light up the world.

# What Gods Are These?

*I*t was a message that began to spread now all along the eastern coast of the Mediterranean Sea, and particularly to the city of Antioch, whose proud, Greek citizens looked down upon the early members of the church and made fun of them. "What shall we call these peculiar people?" they asked one another. "Christians, I suppose," said someone in Antioch; and from that time on, the followers of Jesus had that name.

Saul had come to be known and trusted in time by the Christians in Jerusalem, but the young church was in great trouble in that city. The grandson of Herod the Great was now in power, and he persecuted the new sect relentlessly. James the brother of John was beheaded; Peter was arrested and once more miraculously escaped. It was clear that Saul would not survive long in Jerusalem, and so he made his way north to Antioch. There he preached for a year with his good friend Barnabas, and when that community was well established, the two went on a ship together, to bring the Good News to other lands. By this time, Saul had changed his name, and he was now known as Paul the Apostle.

To Cyprus and then into the hills of Asia Minor they traveled, speaking always with the Jews in each community first; but if the Jews would not pay attention to them, then they turned to the pagans and taught them about the kingdom of Jesus Christ. "This

is what God has commanded us to do," said Paul. "For it is
written in our Scriptures,

> *I have made you a light for all nations,*
> *So my salvation may reach the ends of the earth."*

Now, it was hard for many people in these faraway regions to understand what manner of men these were. One day in the land of Lycaonia, a curious crowd had gathered around Paul and Barnabas, and there was among them a man whose feet had been crippled since birth. As he listened to Paul's preaching, new hope suddenly entered the man's heart, and he stared straight at Paul until the apostle noticed him. *This one has the faith to be healed*, thought Paul. So he said in a loud voice to him, "Get to your feet, man—stand up!" And the man immediately stood up and began to walk about, perfectly well.

When the crowd saw this, they began to cry out in their own language, "Look! These men are gods!" And because they knew only the Greek gods in that place, they said of Barnabas, "This must be Zeus!" That was because he was taller and better-looking than Paul; and of Paul they said, "This one is Hermes!" for Hermes was the messenger of the gods. Now the priests rushed out to bring oxen from their temple, all garlanded for a sacrifice to the two men, and Paul and Barnabas were horrified. "You must not do this!" they cried. "Look, we are only human beings like you. Do not bow down to us! We want you to worship the living God, who made all things!" So they ran through the crowd, shouting and protesting with all their might, but even so they were barely able to persuade the people and to prevent the sacrifice. Soon after this, the same people suddenly turned against Paul and Barnabas. Coming to the conclusion that they were wicked men after all, they drove the two apostles away with stones, and left them for dead.

# Council at Jerusalem

A difficult question arose now among the early Christians. More and more non-Jews wanted to join their number; and some of the faithful argued that they should not be admitted unless they were circumcised in obedience to the covenant of Abraham. A meeting was called

in Jerusalem, and there the people heard the ideas of their leaders, Peter and Paul especially, and Jesus' brother James.

"God knows all hearts, and he sees no difference between us," Peter said. "The uncircumcised pagan is purified by his faith in our Lord. I have seen this happen myself!" And next, Paul told of the pagans so gratefully receiving the Good News on his travels abroad.

Then James said, "My brothers, the Scriptures say that the House of David shall be rebuilt, and then all pagans shall turn to God. Let us not make things any more difficult for the foreigners. It is we who were chosen to save them, after all!"

So it was decided that a letter should be sent out to all churches in outlying districts, with a message of warm reassurance to those who had worried over this problem. Christians should always lead a decent life, the letter told them, and they should not insult the ancient God of Israel. Nevertheless, a pagan who believed in Jesus Christ did not have to be circumcised. Like the Jew who also believed, he would find salvation in his faith.

# Mission to Greece

In the council at Jerusalem it had been decided that Paul should be the one to bring Christ's word to the people of foreign nations, and this was a happy choice. Although he suffered often from physical illness, Paul was a brave man and a bold traveler; and he had the gift of making friends wherever he went. He was also one of the world's greatest letter writers, although it must be said that he did not always speak in public very well. Sometimes he became so excited by what he was saying that he quite forgot himself; and one night in Asia Minor he went on preaching so long that a man who sat listening in an upper window finally dozed off, fell three stories down, and broke his neck. Paul stopped long enough to heal him, and then went right on preaching until dawn.

But of all Paul's talents the greatest was his wise and compassionate way of approaching new people in terms of their own beliefs. He did not go to a place like Athens and begin by saying, "You Greeks are stupid to worship gods and goddesses! You had better be baptized in the name of Jesus Christ right away!" Instead, he walked quietly into the city and looked around at everything; and then he took up the Greek custom of arguing about matters of importance every afternoon in the marketplace.

With Paul on this journey was Luke, his close friend and beloved physician, and Luke wrote later, "The favorite amusement of the Greeks at this time, aside from arguing, was listening to lectures on all the latest ideas." Paul had perceived this, of course, and it was not long before he had an invitation for himself

to give a lecture before the council of the Areopagus.

"Men of Athens," said Paul, "I can see that you are very correct and careful about religious matters, for I have been strolling about admiring the many fine monuments in your great city. And I noticed that you have one altar which is inscribed, 'To an Unknown God.' Well, the God you do not know is the very one I want to talk about; and as you see, you have been worshiping him already!"

In this way Paul continued, teaching the Greeks about God the Creator, a power far too great to be contained in any shrine or idol: for it is he in whom all persons live and move and have their being. "We are all God's children," said Paul. "From now on he wants people of every nation to reach out to him, and know him better." Then he began to tell them about Jesus, and how he had been crucified and raised from the dead. At this, there was loud laughter from some in the audience; yet, others said to Paul when he finished speaking, "We think you are saying something important, and we would like to hear more about it." And so, in time, Paul gathered disciples around him in Athens, and also in many other parts of Greece; everywhere in that land, little churches were beginning to spring up.

There was always danger, and there were times of deep discouragement as well. Paul was often beaten and otherwise mistreated, and many times on his travels he landed in jail. As he had behaved like a Greek in the marketplace of Athens, so he took advantage of being a Roman citizen when, in a northern town, he was arrested by officials of Rome. "How dare you have me flogged and locked up without a trial?" cried Paul. "It is against the law to do that to any citizen of the Roman Empire—and I am one!" The local officials were astonished to hear this, and they begged him to leave town quietly. "I will not leave quietly," said Paul. So they had to make a formal apology to him and give him an escort out of town. And this turned out to be quite embarrassing to the officials, because Paul had made Christians of his jailers overnight. As he left, they were all singing hymns and shouting the praises of Jesus Christ!

Some of Paul's happiest days were spent in the Greek city of Corinth. There he found good friends, especially a couple named Priscilla and Aquila, who were soon baptized. Aquila was a tentmaker. This had been Paul's own occupation, and so in Corinth he, too, worked as a tentmaker, and they settled down for a year and a half together in that beautiful city by the sea. Beginning as usual with debates in the synagogue, Paul tried to persuade the Jews that Jesus was the Christ, but they bitterly rejected him. "Do not be silenced," the Lord said to Paul then in a vision. "I am with you, and you will find many people in this city who are on my side."

So Paul spoke boldly to the pagans around him, and they listened. Before long there was a thriving Christian community in Corinth among the Greeks. "You were a logical people," Paul wrote to them later. "You expected to hear a cool and reasonable message from me; but to you, I preached Christ crucified. And that is because God's foolishness is wiser than any human wisdom; and it is because the weakness of God is stronger than any human strength. I serve the Lord, yet I shall be poor and struggling always; for I am glad to be a fool for Christ!"

# Riot at Ephesus

The vast crowd in the stadium at Ephesus was in a fury. "Great is the goddess Diana of the Ephesians!" they roared. When a speaker tried to calm them, they began shouting the same words even more loudly; and they continued to do this for two full hours.

Demetrius the silversmith was leading the riot. He had

worked himself into a rage over the new group of people called Christians; and he especially hated their leader, who had recently come to stay with them—a stubborn and persistent little man named Paul.

Year after year from all over the civilized world, worshipers of the goddess had traveled to Demetrius' city. The temple of Diana at Ephesus was one of the world's great wonders, and after pilgrims had paid homage there, they bought many fine souvenirs to take home with them: little silver images of the goddess, and of her shrine. At festival times Demetrius the silversmith made a great deal of money. So did his friends; and they counted on this as a fact of life.

But the Christians were going about saying that little silver idols were not important. They were teaching the people about a very different sort of God. *Our city will be ruined!* thought Demetrius. Then he saw Paul standing quietly at the edge of the crowd. Evidently the man was not going to be heard at all, today. Demetrius laughed, and began shouting once more, "Diana! Great is the goddess of Ephesus!"

# Prison on a Hilltop

**P**aul sat looking out over the blue curve of the bay at Ephesus. He was in prison again, but by now he was getting used to it. The walls around him sometimes served to protect him from his enemies, and the silence of his long hours in captivity gave him time for prayer. Messages were coming to him constantly from the new churches in Asia Minor and abroad, and he wrote letter after letter back to them. In each place, people were having different kinds of problems—and turning to Paul for the solutions to them all. Like a mother hen, he worried and fretted over each little community; and like an eagle in his eyrie, he gazed far out over the world as a whole, seeking the patterns of thought and action that must shape the future of his mission for Christ.

He sighed and shook his head. How sad it was that people still wanted worldly power, so that even Christians quarreled among themselves about which one had the best leader, or the best way of preaching or of praying, or the best church. Did they not understand that the world was surely coming to an end, and Jesus Christ was coming in glory to judge them all? What would all of their self-importance matter then?

They quarreled endlessly too, it seemed, over all sorts of rules and regulations. Each one wanted Paul to say that his own ideas were right and the ideas of his neighbor were nonsense.

Very well, then, rules were necessary, and Paul would do his best to sort them out. But all of this was so far from the main point! Had they forgotten the teachings of their Lord and King already? Had they forgotten that Jesus of Nazareth had shown them in his own life how to live?

Surely it was time, Paul thought, for someone to begin writing down the whole story of Jesus' life and teachings. He must speak to Luke about that. Paul took up his pen. *Jesus died for you,* he wrote. *You are not your own property; you have been bought and paid for on the Cross. You must understand that your bodies are members, that they are parts of a whole, that together they make up the body of Christ.* Do we really need more than this, Paul wondered, to help us make decent rules for daily behavior?

Yet some of the new Christians thought they were better than others, because they had visions or spoke in tongues; and others argued that healing miracles were more important; and still others claimed that they were more virtuous, because they raised money to help the poor. In fact, the real problem was that they were all human beings, so accustomed to struggling against one another that they still could not understand the New Way. But Jesus gave his life to show us how all human beings may become one, and live in peace together. I must try again and again, Paul thought, to teach them that. And he began to write:

*I appeal to you, my dear brothers, for the sake of our Lord Jesus Christ: Make up your quarrels! You are all given different gifts, but they come from the same Spirit. If one of you can preach wisely, that comes from the Spirit. And if another has the*

*gift of faith, that comes from the Spirit too. And if one can heal, it is through the Spirit; and if another can prophesy, or speak in tongues, then all of these are the work of the same Spirit, who gives different gifts to different people for a good reason.*

*It is just as a body is made up of different parts. If all the parts were the same, how could it be a body? If your whole body were just an eye, how could you hear anything? If it were all just an ear, how could you smell anything? God put all the separate parts of the body there on purpose, so that they might help one another. Your eye cannot say to your hand, "I do not need you!" In the same way, you people all need to work together. You are all necessary parts of Christ's body, which is his church.*

Since the day on the road to Damascus, Paul had wondered many times why that great miracle of light had come to him. Surely, of all people on earth at that moment, he had been the most unworthy. He had learned then, above all things, the power of love. It had made him into a new person, and if he did nothing else with his life now, this was what he must teach to others. *Though I speak with the tongues of men and of angels,* he wrote, *if I speak without love, I am like sounding brass and tinkling cymbals. If I have the gift of prophecy, and if I know all things, and if I have the faith that moves mountains—still, if I do not love, I am nothing at all. Love is patient and kind; it is never jealous. Love does not boast; it is never rude. Love is not selfish; it is always ready to excuse, to trust, to hope, to endure whatever happens. Of all things you must learn, dear friends, know this: There are only three things on earth of lasting value: faith, hope, and love. And the greatest of these by far is love.*

# If God Be with Me

The ship was waiting in the harbor. Once again Paul was going back to Jerusalem, and this time, parting from his friends was hard indeed. "Guard yourselves well," he said as he embraced the weeping elders from the church at Ephesus, and kissed them one by one. He had been with them

for three long, difficult years; and now they all knew that they would never see one another again.

For a long time Paul had been preaching in the eastern Mediterranean, but his thoughts had turned more and more often of late to Rome. There, in the stronghold of the Empire, a little group of Christians lived. He knew that he must go to them and bear witness to the Lord in the world's greatest city. The danger would be serious, but the danger of this work was great everywhere.

As his ship moved out to sea, Paul turned his face into the wind. *If God be with me, who can be against me?* he thought. He had written those words recently, in a letter to Rome. Then, with rising joy, he remembered something else from the letter: words of comfort that had come to him one night, deep in prayer. *For I am convinced,* he repeated once more to himself, *that neither death, nor life, nor angels, nor principalities, nor powers, nor height, nor depth, nor anything created or anything yet to come, can ever separate us from the love of God which is in Christ Jesus, our Lord.*

# Appeal to Caesar

L uke the physician was traveling with Paul again, and taking careful note of all that happened along the way. From port to port they ventured north together, and then overland from Caesarea to Jerusalem. How good it was to see their friends in the Holy City, and to worship once more in that magnificent Temple! Luke, of all people, knew that Paul was in grave danger, but even he was surprised by the violence of it when it struck.

Paul had been in the city only twelve days when some Jews from Asia suddenly began shouting at him in the Temple, accusing him of doing and saying all manner of things that were against their Law. The mood of the city was so tense just now that, in no time, an angry mob gathered. They dragged Paul from the Temple and would have beaten him to death then and there if a Roman officer had not come with soldiers to rescue him. "What has the man done?" Lysias, the Roman officer, asked the people. But their shouts of response were so confused that he could make no sense of it; and when Paul tried to address them, they only became more furious.

So Lysias brought Paul into the Roman fort and had him stripped and bound down for a lashing. But Paul said, "It is against your own law for you to do this! I have had no trial, and I am a Roman citizen!" Lysias was frightened when he heard this, and he set Paul free immediately. He ordered the chief priests and leaders of the Jews to hold a meeting and examine Paul themselves.

The next day, Paul spoke boldly before the Sanhedrin.

"Before God I have a clear conscience," he said. "I am on trial here only because I am a Pharisee and so believe in the resurrection of the dead." When he said this, the Pharisees in the hall began fighting with the Sadducees over the question of resurrection, and another riot broke out. Again the Romans had to rescue Paul and bring him back to their fort.

Now a group of forty citizens of Jerusalem took a solemn vow that they would neither eat nor drink until they had murdered Paul. Fortunately, his nephew heard of the plot and came to Lysias. The Roman took quick action. Under heavy guard he sent Paul out of the city and delivered him to the governor, Felix of Caesarea.

The chief priests sent a delegation to Caesarea now, and their lawyer, Tertullus, argued that Paul should be punished for being a troublemaker and a Nazarene, for this was what the early Christians were called in Jerusalem. But Paul argued convincingly that he was faithful to the God of his ancestors and that he had committed no crime. Felix could not decide what to do with him. In the end, he did not make any decision at all; he simply kept Paul under house arrest until his term as governor was up, and then he turned him over to Festus, the new governor. Meantime he had a number of long talks with Paul about the New Way of Jesus' followers; but the more he heard, the more he decided that he himself did not want to behave so well as all that.

Festus was very much interested in the prisoner. He saw immediately that the Jews were determined to do away with him, but because Paul was a Roman citizen, he offered him the full protection of Roman law. "I appeal to Caesar," Paul told him.

And Festus replied, "Very well, then, to Caesar you shall go."

A few days after this, King Agrippa himself came to visit Festus. And Festus said to him, "I have a man here who is in trouble with the local authorities. They want to do away with him, but I have told them that Romans are not in the habit of delivering up a man without a fair trial. It is some quarrel or other over their own religion, having to do with a dead man called Jesus, who, this man Paul says, is still alive." King Agrippa was intrigued. "I should like to hear Paul myself," he said. And so, the next day, Paul was brought before the king in solemn assembly. "Tell us about yourself, so that I can make a report to Caesar," Festus ordered him.

Paul began with the story of his youth as a strict and devoted Pharisee; and he told how at first he had persecuted the followers of Jesus. Then he told of the day when Jesus himself had come to him in a blinding light and changed his life entirely. "After that, King Agrippa," he said, "I could not disobey the vision from heaven. And from that day on I have testified to the truth, which is exactly what the prophets and Moses himself said would happen: that the Christ would suffer and die, and be raised up again. And that, as the first to conquer death, he would proclaim the light that shines for our people now, and for all nations."

At this point Festus cried out, "Paul, you are out of your mind! All this learning of yours has driven you to madness!" But Paul replied, "I am not mad. The king understands these matters! You believe in the prophets, sir, do you not?"

And the king replied, "A little more of this, and I think you might make a Christian out of me."

# Voyage to Rome

**K**ing Agrippa thought it over carefully, and then he said to Festus, the governor, "This man is doing nothing to deserve death or punishment. Actually, he could be set free here and now, but for the fact that he has appealed to Caesar." In view of that, it was decided to send Paul to Rome.

He went as a prisoner, but Luke was allowed to accompany him; and he was treated with courtesy by the centurion, named Julius, who was in charge for the first stage of the journey. The winds were unfavorable, however, and their little ship struggled along very slowly past the island of Cyprus and up the Asian coast. In Lycia, Julius found a ship that was leaving for Italy, and he bade them farewell and put them aboard.

Again they set sail toward the west, and again the winds were against them. Taking shelter on the lee shore of Crete, they considered their situation. "It is too late in the season," said Paul. "This voyage will be very dangerous." They should have stayed in a safe harbor for the winter, but the centurion now in charge would not listen to Paul, or to the ship's captain, either. And so they set off once more.

And now from the northeast a winter tempest burst in full fury upon them, driving the ship helplessly before it, toward the middle of the Mediterranean Sea. Two hundred seventy-six people were on board, and the ship was heavily laden as well with cargo, provisions, and gear. The sailors bound cables around the ship as best they could, and threw out a sea anchor. Still they sped on, pitching and wallowing fearfully, under a sky so dark with storm clouds that they saw neither sun nor stars, day after day. Water began pouring over the sides; the sailors threw the cargo overboard, trying to save the ship, and then they jettisoned all of the ship's gear. Everyone was mortally frightened, and even Luke had given up all hope of survival, when Paul stood up among the men to speak.

"Take courage, friends," he said. "The God I serve has sent me an angel, telling me that all who sail with me now shall be safe, for I am destined to go before Caesar. Only the ship will be

lost, and we will be stranded on an island, but no one will be hurt, or die."

On the fourteenth night, the crew sensed that land was near. Taking soundings, they found that they were indeed in shallow water, and now they were fearful that they might strike a reef in the dark. "Come now," Paul said to them. "Let us break bread together. You have been too troubled to eat for a long time, and you will be needing your strength." Then he took bread, and gave thanks, and they shared it. Soon afterward it was daybreak; they saw they were near a beach, and tried to run the ship up on it. But they struck on rocks and were trapped there; and then the waves began pounding the ship apart.

"Kill the prisoners!" the sailors cried, thinking that they might

swim away and escape. But the centurion would not let them do it, for he was determined to bring Paul to Caesar; and they all made their way, swimming and floating on pieces of the wreckage, safely to shore.

They discovered in a short time that they were now on the island of Malta, quite a few miles south of Italy. "The inhabitants there treated us with unusual kindness," Luke wrote later. "They made us all welcome and lit a huge fire on the beach for us, for it had begun to rain again, and the weather was very cold." Paul was carrying a bundle of sticks he had collected for the fire when it happened that a poisonous viper crawled out of the bundle and clung to his hand. When the natives of Malta saw this, they said, "Look at that man! He must be a murderer. He has escaped the sea, but Divine Justice is going to punish him anyway." But then they saw Paul shake the viper from his hand into the fire, and when they saw that he was walking about after that perfectly well, they decided that he must be a god!

Paul and Luke were received, after this, by the governor of that district, whose name was Publius, and hospitably entertained at his estate. When Paul saw that the father of Publius was lying ill in bed with a fever, he laid his hands upon him, saying a prayer. The old man was healed, and after this, the people of the island brought many others who were sick to be healed by Paul also. And after three more months, with many gifts and many tokens of respect from the islanders, Paul and Luke sailed away, bound once more for the city of Rome.

So after many years of hope, having imagined it many times over again, Paul arrived at last at the seat of the Empire, the center of the known world's political power. The chain he still wore, and the house arrest that was still imposed upon him, did little to keep him from doing the work he wanted to do there. Luke's account tells us that a little band of Christians came out several miles from the city to give him a warm welcome, and that he waited only three days before beginning to discuss the Way of Jesus with people from the synagogue in Rome. He does not tell us of Paul's appearance before Caesar, and it may be that a formal trial never took place, for lack of witnesses. For two years, Luke says, Paul lived peacefully in Rome in his own rented lodgings, and welcomed all those who came to visit him. He preached the Way of Christ and taught without hindrance during the entire time of his captivity.

The rest of Paul's history must be pieced together from the work of other writers. It is believed that he, as well as the apostle Peter, suffered death as a martyr to Christianity during the reign of the vicious Emperor Nero, in Rome.

But the story of Paul's faith is never-ending, for we also have his letters. In them, we hear him explaining his ideas, expressing his hopes, chiding and coaxing his friends, arranging his travels —and above all, telling the spiritual truths that had become the very center of his being. A letter to a young man named Timothy serves as a fitting close to that story. It is filled with affection and concern for Timothy and his friends, and then Paul writes:

*As for me, the time has come for me to depart. I have fought the good fight to the end; I have run the race to the finish; I have kept the faith. There is nothing more to come for me except the crown of victory that Jesus Christ will give to me—and not only to me, but to all of those who long for the Day when he will come again.*

# Revelation

S ome years later, on the island of Patmos, where the Roman overlords kept rebels and criminals at hard labor, there was a prisoner named John who had been sent there for preaching the word of Jesus Christ. One day, John heard the sound of a great trumpet behind him, and when he turned around, he saw the heavens opening to him in an enormous vision sent by God.

Jesus stood beside him, shining like the morning star, and he said to John, "Do not be afraid. It is I, who was dead and am now alive again forever and ever; and I am the Alpha and the Omega, the First and the Last, the Beginning and the End." Then Jesus showed him all that would happen in times to come; and John saw that there would be war in heaven, and that the evil powers of the earth would all be brought down to destruction. And he saw that after the very end of the world itself, there would be a New Jerusalem, more beautiful than anything that mankind had ever built, where all the faithful would rise up in glory and dwell together in everlasting peace.

God showed himself to John upon a throne of jeweled light, with the colors of the rainbow blazing all around him, and in his hand he held a scroll sealed with seven seals. Only the Lamb, who had been sacrificed and raised up from the dead again, was powerful enough to open up the seals; and John understood

from this that Jesus rules over human history. As the seals were opened, he saw the Four Horsemen of the Apocalypse striding forth: the white horse of Conquest bearing the Victor with his crown, the red horse of War, the black horse of Famine, and the pale horse of Plague. These were the forces that brought ruin to any empire that oppressed God's people, as Babylon had done in ages past—and now the power that would surely fall was Rome.

"Tell my saints that they will be comforted," said Jesus. "Those who love me shall be given hidden manna, and each one shall have a white stone with a new name upon it, known only to God and the one who receives it. And the time will come when my people will never hunger or thirst again, and the sun and scorching wind will never plague them. For the Lamb who is at the throne will be their Shepherd, and will lead them to springs of living water; and God will wipe away all tears from their eyes."

When the seventh seal was broken, there was silence in the sanctuary of heaven. Then seven angels blew seven trumpets, one by one, and the wrath of God descended upon the earth. This was Armageddon, where the wicked who had not repented would be utterly destroyed. Fire and earthquake struck; the whole sky smoked and thundered; and all the cities, all the islands, and all the mountains of the world fell down to darkness and disappeared.

Yet that was not the end of it, for John saw a great war after that, led by the archangel Michael and all the hosts of heaven against a monstrous beast who dwelled in the abyss. The beast had been given his power by Satan, and he had gathered all the armies of the wicked kings and emperors on earth to fight the warriors of God. The beast was captured, together with the false prophet who helped him to do his evil work; and the two of them were thrown into a fiery pit of burning sulphur, to be held captive there for a thousand years.

And now before his wondering eyes John saw a new heaven, and a new earth. An angel came to him and brought his spirit to the top of a great mountain, where he could look out upon the City of God, which was glittering and blazing like a diamond in the high, pure light. There were twelve gates to the City, one for each of the twelve tribes of Israel; and there were twelve foundation stones, one bearing the name of each of the twelve apostles of Christ. The streets and buildings of the City were all made of pure gold, transparent as glass; and the gates were made of great pearls; and the walls of the City were shining with precious stones.

Springing from the throne of God and the Lamb, the river of life flowed crystal-clear through the middle of this New Jerusalem, and on either side was the Tree of Life, bearing leaves and fruits throughout the year. And in the City lived those who had been true to God, those whose names had been written in the Book of Life.

"Here is the water of life," said Jesus, "and here is the tree of life, which is the reward for all those who have served me faithfully. Let all those who thirst come to me, and I will be their God, and they will be as my own children to me."

John wrote down all this, and far more, for the Christians who were under his care in Asia; and with these words he ended the book of Revelation:

*Amen; come, Lord Jesus. May the grace*
*of the Lord be with you all. Amen.*

## SANDOL STODDARD

is well known to readers of all ages as the author of fourteen books for young people (including the prize-winning *Saint George and the Dragon*, *Five Who Found the Kingdom*, *Growing Time*, and the perennial best seller *I Like You*) and as a leading writer and lecturer on the hospice concept whose book on this subject, *The Hospice Movement: A Better Way of Caring for the Dying*, is regarded as definitive. For service to the hospice cause, she received special recognition from St. Christopher's Hospice, London, and the Humanitarian Award of the Forbes Health System in the United States. She has edited the journal, *Spiritual Journeys*, and has served on the boards of several interfaith organizations.

A *magna cum laude* graduate of Bryn Mawr and the mother of four grown sons, she now lives and writes the year round on Martha's Vineyard, enjoying visits from her family and friends from around the world.

## TONY CHEN

is one of America's foremost watercolorists, with a long list of honors, publications, and one-man shows. His paintings are in many museums and private collections throughout the country and have won awards from the Society of Illustrators, The American Institute of Graphic Arts, and the Children's Book Showcase. He has written and illustrated two books for children and illustrated over forty more.

Born in Jamaica, West Indies, he came to the United States in 1949 and received a B.F.A. with honors from Pratt Institute, Brooklyn. He now lives and works in Corona, New York.